DECISION MAKING IN STATUTORY REVIEWS ON CHILDREN IN CARE

Decision Making in Statutory Reviews on Children in Care

RUTH SINCLAIR
Loughborough University

Gower

Published by
Gower Publishing Company Limited, Gower House, Croft Road,
Aldershot, Hampshire GU11 3HR, England

and

Gower Publishing Company, Old Post Road, Brookfield,
Vermont 05036, U.S.A.

British Library Cataloguing in Publication Data

Sinclair, Ruth
  Decision making in statutory reviews on children in care.
  1. Children---Institutional care---England---Decision making
  2. Children---Institutional care---Law and legislation---
  England   I. Title
  362.7'32'0942   HV887.G7

Library of Congress Cataloging in Publication Data

Sinclair, Ruth.
  Decision making in statutory reviews on children in care.

  Bibliography: p.
1. Children--legal status, laws, etc.--Great Britain.
2. Foster home care--law and legislation--Great Britain.
3. Custody of children--Great Britain. 4. Child welfare--
Great Britain--decision making.   I. Title.
KD3305.S53 1984   344.10432733   84-10298

ISBN 0-566-00757-6

Printed and bound in Great Britain by
Antony Rowe Limited, Chippenham.

Contents

Acknowledgements

This research, which was financed by the Department of Health and Social Security, was undertaken in the Department of Social Sciences, Loughborough University of Technology. The research was supervised throughout by Professor Adrian Webb. I wish to express my thanks to Professor Webb for his support and help both with the research itself and the preparation of this book.

I am greatly indebted to Wainshire Social Services Department for enabling me to undertake this research. I am particularly grateful to the members of the three Social Work Area Teams and the staff of the Children's Homes who participated in the research. Their generosity with their time and their willing co-operation made the empirical work particularly enjoyable.

I wish to thank both Adoption and Fostering and Community Care for permission to reproduce material which was first published in those journals.

Lastly, I wish to express my thanks to Max Hunt from the Loughborough University Computer Centre for his patient assistance with the computer analysis, to Gwen Moon for her equally patient typing throughout the research project and to Mandy Wilcox for her co-operation and care in typing the manuscript for this book.

1 The development of child care policy

INTRODUCTION

The development of the child care policies in Britain since
the war is characterised by a series of parliamentary acts
which resulted from an expressed dissatisfaction or concern
with existing services. These dissatisfactions were the
subject for enquiries and reports which in turn resulted in
new legislation. Thus, in the 1940's, the death of foster
child Dennis O'Neill was followed by the Curtis Committee
(HMSO, 1946) and the 1948 Children Act. In the 1950's rising
delinquency rates lead to the establishment of the Ingleby
Committee. However, as part of its brief it was also asked
to consider "whether local authorities should be given new
powers and duties to prevent or forestall the suffering of
children through neglect in their own homes". In the event,
it was this aspect of their report which had most lasting
impact, by acknowledging the need for 'preventative' social
work. The findings from this committee, when it eventually
reported (HMSO, 1960) became the basis for the 1963 Children
and Young Persons Act. In the 1960's the continuing concern
with the substantial increase in levels of juvenile delinquency lead to two white papers, 'The Child and the Family and
the Young Offender' in 1965 and 'Children in Trouble' in 1968.
It was the latter which became the model for the 1969 Children
and Young Persons Act. In the 1970's the child care services
were faced with a series of very damaging reports on child
deaths, the most explosive being the report into the death of
Maria Colwell (HMSO, 1974). This, together with the Houghton
Report on Adoption of Children (HMSO, 1972), provided much of
the impetus for the 1975 Children Act.

  Each of these new Acts brought about major changes in the
organisational structure and administrative procedures for
dealing with children in need of care and protection. Each of
these acts also, to some extent, represented a compromise
between conflicting assumptions, values and aims for child
care practice which may well explain why the same problems so

1

often reappear. As Packman says in her study of child care policy in Britain:

> despite all these changes and some palpable improvements in service, we are now faced with many of the same problems and failures with which the era began ... standards of child care practice are as much in question now as they were then. (Packman, 1981).

Indeed once again in 1983 we have a government enquiry into Children in Care, this time in the form of a Select Committee of the House of Commons. Unfortunately the deliberations of this committee were interrupted by the parliamentary general election of June 1983. Although it has been suggested that this committee may be reconstituted in 1984 in a much reduced form, it is very unlikely that it will produce the substantial report that was originally expected.

The present position on children in care can best be appreciated through an understanding of the changes that have occurred over the last forty years in the legal and administrative framework, in the knowledge base and in the emphases and trends in child care practice. Hence we shall start this research report with a brief summary of such developments.

THE CHILDREN ACT, 1948

The attitude to child care that was inherited by the new Children's Departments, when they were created in 1948, was largely one of 'salvationism' - whereby children were viewed as being in need of protection from the inadequacies and undesirable influence of unsatisfactory parents, and in need of training in social and vocational skills in order to achieve an early independence. There was a mood of optimism that children could be rescued from unsatisfactory homes and directed to a new and better life, in particular through foster care (BASW, 1983). Thus much of the work of the early Children's Officers was in the development of foster care; in the finding of suitable foster homes and the placement in those homes of children who had been separated from their natural parents: a policy of 'rescue and remove'. The requirements of the new service to meet the needs of deprived children had to be learnt step by step. In particular, one aspect of this service reflected a new departure: a commitment to a personal service - so that each child in care would have its individual needs looked after by a Child Care Officer.

THE CHILDREN AND YOUNG PERSONS ACT, 1963

Although the major emphasis in the early work of the Children's Departments was on the need to improve standards of substitute care, it became increasingly apparent to the Children's Officers that more attention needed to be placed on prevention - both prevention of the separation of a child from its family and prevention of neglect and cruelty within the family. Many Children's Departments did take initiatives in this direction, but many were hampered by a lack of any resources for preventative work and a lack of cooperation with other agencies, particularly housing departments. These initiatives in providing resources and facilities to vulnerable families were eventaully given statutory recognition in the 1963 Children and Young Persons Act, which placed a duty upon local authorities:

> to make available such advice, guidance and assistance as may promote the welfare of children by diminishing the need to receive children into or keep them in care ... any provisions made by a local authority under this subsection may include provision for giving assistance in kind, or, in exceptional circumstances, in cash.

This new emphasis on prevention led to an important shift in the focus of the child care service. The cases of children supervised in their own homes were soon to greatly outnumber those of children 'in care', as both the scale and the range of services to families expanded. Part of this expansion was the growing involvement of child care officers with juvenile delinquents or young people at risk of becoming delinquent. Packman (1981) gives a detailed account of the work of the Oxfordshire Children's Department in developing policies to deal with young offenders. Many such initiatives influenced the thinking behind the 1969 Children and Young Persons Act. Packman says, "local experiment had become national policy".

THE CHILDREN AND YOUNG PERSONS ACT, 1969

There were two opposing philosophies on the appropriate way to deal with young offenders. One school of thought saw delinquent children as no different from deprived children, except they were in trouble with the law; both were victims of poor environmental backgrounds or of neglectful, often broken, homes and therefore in need of care and protection. The other school saw the young delinquent as an offender, who must suffer the due process of law and whose behaviour must be subject to training and control. The 1969 Act was an attempt to reconcile these views. This almost impossible task was made even more difficult by the changes made to the original package by the new Conservative government before implementation took place. Briefly, the Act removed the distinction between children who came before the courts because of unsatisfactory home circumstances and those who had committed an offence: both could be made subject to a Care Order, which gave the choice of residence of the child to the Social Service Department. The duty which the Act placed upon local authorities and the courts to develop strategies to deal with these young people in the community was to be fulfilled by the introduction of Intermediate Treatment.

Effective implementation of the Act was however hindered by the confusion which followed the reorganisation of local government services in 1971. Although most people welcomed the new Social Services Departments as a continuation of the move towards a more integrated, broad based, family approach to the personal social services, the process of reorganisation had an almost paralysing effect on much social work. The skills and training of the old child care officers were diluted in the expanded service. This, together with acute shortage of residential accommodation, meant that the early years of the operation of the 1969 Act lead to much criticism of social workers by magistrates and police. Indeed, throughout much of the 1970's social work as a whole was faced with a 'bad press'. Despite some examples of exciting developments in child care practice such as the special family placement project in Kent (Hazel, 1981) and other specialist fostering schemes (Shaw & Hipgrave, 1983), the general picture of social work was of overloaded, generic, often young, case workers, with increasing statutory responsibilities: a situation which encouraged a move away from a family or community centred approach back to individually focused and crisis orientated work, although still following, theoretically, a policy of prevention and rehabilitation.

THE CHILDREN ACT, 1975

The concerns and controversies that had arisen within child care are well illustrated by three events which occurred in 1973. These were: the death of Maria Colwell; the publication of an American book 'Beyond the Best Interests of the Child, (Goldstein, Freud and Solnit, 1973); the research findings published in 'Children Who Wait' (Rowe and Lambert, 1973). Each of these events was influential in the debate which preceded the passing of the 1975 Children Act, and we shall briefly consider them in turn.

Maria Colwell died at the hands of her step father, having been returned by the Social Services Department to live with her natural mother after six years in a seemingly happy foster home. Maria's death and the subsequent enquiry were to receive maximum press publicity. The enquiry team said "What has clearly emerged, at least to us, is a failure of a system" (DHSS, 1974). However, much criticism was also expressed of the decision by the Social Services Department to allow Maria to be returned to her mother, a situation which highlighted the lack of security of foster placements. One of the strongest criticisms of the handling of the case came in a book 'Remember Maria', in which the author accused social workers of being too strongly influenced by notions of maternal deprivation and giving too great a prominence to the 'blood-tie' relationship. Adherence to such attitudes, he suggested, resulted in the adoption of policies of rehabilitation without sufficient thought being given to the child's best interests (Howells, 1974).

A similar theme was prominent in the influential study, 'Beyond the Best Interests of the Child' (Goldstein, Freud and Solnit, 1973). These authors believed that what was important to a child was his 'psychological parents', that is, the parents to whom he had an emotional attachment - an attachment which resulted, not from biological ties but rather from day-to-day interaction in a caring and sharing relationship. Furthermore this study suggested that children were incapable of loving two sets of parents, especially if they were hostile to each other. Therefore continuity and security were seen as vital to a child and the authors argued that this should be reflected in placement decisions.

The third influential event in 1973 was the publication of a study which had been undertaken on behalf of ABAFA by Rowe and Lambert. In contrast to official policy this study pointed to the fact that many children stayed in care, often in residential establishments for most of their childhood; furthermore, once a child had been in care for six months he had only a one in four chance of returning to his family. Rowe and Lambert found that from a sample of children under eleven years old, who had already been in care for six months, 22% were thought by their social workers to be in need of a permanent substitute family. These then are the 'Children Who Wait' - children who are inappropriately placed and who are 'waiting' for a decision that will place them more appropriately. Why do so many children 'wait'? Lack of resources is obviously one cause, but Rowe and Lambert concluded that lack of commitment to long-term planning and poor quality decision-making were also vitally important factors.

All these studies pointed to a need for greater protection for children from irresponsible parents and for children in care to be provided with greater security. Perhaps even as Adcock et al suggest "children might well need as much protection from inadequate local authority care as from their birth parent" (Adcock, White and Rowland, 1983).

By no means did everyone accept that local authorities should be given increased powers which would restrict those of natural parents. Thorpe (1974) argued that natural parents were not given the necessary social work support to maintain contact with their children, and indeed social workers often discouraged contact. Yet there is evidence of the crucial role of social work activity in the successful rehabilitation of children (Aldgate 1977, 1980). Holman argued for the development of 'inclusive' rather than 'exclusive' fostering, whereby a foster parent could work with both the social worker and the natural parents to facilitate the rehabilitation of the child, if at all possible. (Holman, 1975). Others stressed the links between poverty, homelessness, social deprivation and the receipt of children into care. (CPAG, 1975; Wilson, 1974). Indeed BASW joined with four other organisations, NCOPF, CPAG, Gingerbread and MIND, in issuing a joint statement because they were concerned that children were coming into care because of social deprivation or lack of preventative social work.

Fox labels these two value positions as the 'kinship defenders' and the 'state-as-parent protagonists' (Fox, 1982) and their differences were very evident in the debate surrounding the passing of the 1975 Children Act.

This Act was wide ranging and its implementation was phased over a lengthy period. Indeed, by early 1984 several parts of the Act have still to be implemented. In general terms the Act gave more power to local authorities to assume parental rights over children in voluntary care; it made the process of adoption easier, even against parental wishes; it gave greater security to placements in substitute care and for the first time it gave children in care the right to be consulted about decisions affecting them. The overriding principle inherent in the implementation of the Act was to be 'the welfare of the child'. It placed the duty upon local authorities, in reaching decisions about a child in their care, to give first consideration to the need to safeguard and promote the child's welfare throughout his childhood.

THE NINETEEN EIGHTIES

Social work in general and child care in particular entered the 1980's in an atmosphere of growing public scepticism about both the purposes and practices of social workers. As Barclay says in the introduction to his report 'Too much is generally expected of social workers. We load upon them unrealistic expectations and we then complain when they do not live up to them' (Barclay, 1982). The Barclay Report was the outcome of an independent enquiry into the 'role and tasks of social workers', requested by the Secretary of State for Social Services because of continuing, underlying uncertainties about the future of social work. Given unfavourable public attitudes, it was reassuring to the profession that Barclay was able to say:

> In spite of all the complexities and uncertainties surrounding the functions of social workers, we are united in our belief that the work they do is of vital importance in our society ... and social workers are needed as never before.

The complexities of the social work task as identified by Barclay are exemplified in the field of child care. The implementation of the 1975 Act has done nothing to reconcile the 'kinship defenders' or the 'state-as-parent protagonists'. If anything a greater polarization of views has occurred which is being crudely characterised in the national and the social work press as parents' rights versus children's rights. While there is a large measure of agreement that the focus should be on the welfare of the child, the controversy surrounds the way in which 'a child's best interest' is defined and the ways of fulfilling that definition.

Although the 1975 Children Act gave the local authority the power to offer greater protection to neglected or abused children, doubts have continued to be expressed over the ability of the local authorities to fulfil a parental role and to offer secure and stable substitute homes to children in their care. These doubts stem from continuing evidence of the failure of Social Service Departments to implement effective long-term plans for children in care. The story of the early life of Graham Gaskin in the care of a local authority is one that resulted from ill considered reactive decision-making, compounded by appalling standards of substitute care (McVeigh, 1981). This is but one vivid personal illustration of the disasters that can befall children allowed to 'drift' in care. It is from consideration of these issues that a 'philosophy of permanence' has been articulated. One of the strongest promoters of this philosophy is the British Agencies for Adoption and Fostering, which sees planning for permanence as a way of avoiding long-term care while recognising the interests of both parents and children.

> The underlying philosophy of the new approach is that children need and have a right to a stable permanent home and should be given the legal security to make this possible. A child in care cannot have a permanent home; permanence can only be achieved if the child has a stable home, either with birth parents or with adoptive parents. (Adcock, White and Rowland, 1983).

The emphasis of this approach is still on a need for rehabilitation and a permanent place for the child with his natural parents, but with a recognised alternative course of action available if the optimum plan is not achieved within a time limit.

Whether in response to such a 'philosophy of permanence', or as a result of pressure from public criticism, the application of the 1975 Act has seen an increase in the use of compulsory powers by the local authorities: increasing assumptions of parental rights over children in voluntary care; increasing use of Care Orders for younger children or children who have committed less serious offences; increasing use of Place of Safety Orders; increasing applications for adoptions without parental consent; increasing use of wardship proceedings.

This greater use, by the local authorities, of formal powers over children and families is subject to increasing challenge from several quarters, in particular the Children's Legal Centre, The Family Rights Centre, and The National Council for One Parent Families. The objections of these organisations are prompted by a concern with the infringement of civil liberties or denials of natural justice that arise from the exercise of the powers of local authorities, for instance in terminating contact between a child and his family, or in assuming parental rights over a child. They argue that such action should only be taken when authorised by the courts, and not through administrative procedures. These arguments have achieved a measure of success: the DHSS issued new draft guidelines on the assumption of parental rights and parental access to children during Autumn 1983.

Simultaneously, pressure continues to give children and young people in care a greater say in decisions that relate to them, which is, after all, a requirement of the 1975 Act. The initiative taken by the National Children's Bureau in their conference for young people in care has lead to the establishment of several Who Cares? groups (Page and Clark, 1977). The National Association of Children and Young People in Care is growing in numbers and experience, giving it the confidence to question the actions of local authorities in dealing with children in their care.

Because of a recognition of the uncertainties, indeed conflicts, surrounding child care law and practice there was a general welcome for the establishment, in 1983, of the enquiry into Children in Care by the House of Commons Select Committee on Social Services and a real sense of disappointment that the Select Committee appears to have been a victim of the 1983 dissolution of parliament. Looking at the development of the child care services since the war, one could ask: is it inevitable that there will be uncertainty and conflict in this area? The situation is certainly full of inherent contradictions. A first choice may be to help keep a child united with his parents, but some parents are not able or willing to provide for the needs of their children. Not only must these children be protected, they must also be offered an alternative that will serve them well throughout the whole of their childhood. As BASW notes: "All too often there's no ideal solution, but rather a question of weighing unsatisfactory options and selecting the least detrimental alternative" (BASW, 1983).

However, one could also ask, is it possible that the conflicts surrounding child care issues are more apparent than real? The polarisation of the argument has lead to a simplification of the discussion so that children in care are treated as a single aggregate, rather than the heterogeneous group that they are. A policy that is appropriate for a very young child is unlikely to serve the needs of a disaffected teenager; nor are the needs of a handicapped child with no parental contact the same as those of a child whose mother is temporarily unable to care for her through illness.

How does this confusion among child care policy makers impact on field social workers? There may be a danger that because of the complexities of the pressures and the undue simplification of the debate that social workers may be inhibited in acting decisively on behalf of their child clients or they may adhere too rigidly to a single vogue practice. It is necessary to ensure that an environment is created in which social workers feel sufficiently secure to be guided in their practice solely by the needs of each individual child.

The discussion in this chapter of both the development and present state of child care policies sets the broad context for an understanding of current child care practices. In the next chapter the discussion will move from this broad consideration of policy issues to focus more narrowly on child care practice and to one aspect of practice in particular, namely statutory reviews.

2 Statutory reviews on children in care

INTRODUCTION

This chapter begins by setting out the statutory requirements
for reviewing the cases of children in care. This is followed
by an examination of some of the existing literature on
reviews, together with a comparison of judicial reviews in the
United States of America, and the Scottish Children's Hearings.
Consideration is then given to the purpose of reviews, and to
recent attempts within the child care field to ensure that
reviews are used more effectively. The chapter concludes with
a short section reporting on the evidence relating to reviews
that was submitted to the House of Commons Select Committee on
Children in Care.

THE STATUTORY BACKGROUND

Section 21 of the 1955 Boarding-Out Regulations requires that
foster placements must be reviewed within three months and
thereafter at least every six months. The general instruction
contained in these regulations is to review "the child's
welfare, conduct, health and progress". (These regulations
are now included under Section 22 Child Care Act, 1980).

Section 27(4) of the Children and Young Persons Act of 1969
amended the law to require reviews to be held every six months
on all children in the care of the Local Authority. If a child
is in care under a Care Order, this Act added an additional
requirement, namely 'to consider in the course of the review
whether to make application for the discharge of the order'.

Apart from the timing of reviews these laws contained no
regulation on the conduct of the review. Section 3, par.7(1)
of the 1975 Children Act (now Section 20 of the 1980 Child
Care Act) gave the Secretary of State the power to make regulations governing statutory reviews by local authorities. This

11

includes the power to make regulations about:

- the manner in which cases are to be reviewed
- the considerations to which local authorities are to
  have regard in reviewing cases
- the time when a child's case is first to be reviewed and
  the frequency of subsequent reviews.

So far no action has been taken on defining or implementing such regulations, although a DHSS circular (LAC(76)15) provides some guidance on the possible nature of such regulations, with reference to:

(a) the timing of reviews
(b) who should be present.

The relevant sections of this circular are quoted below:

(a) A second stage (i.e. after reception into care) for decision would be reached when the child has been in care for between two and four months. Careful planning at this stage for all children may prevent some children from drifting into situations which may not be in their best long-term interests.

(b) Discussions of a child's future should always include parents except where this is obviously inappropriate. Foster parents, residential staff, teachers and other people directly involved in the child's life should also be included in the discussions. A child who is mature enough to understand the implications of such a review could be invited to be present, or at least during part of the discussion at the review. (DHSS/LAC, 1976)

These guidelines carry no statutory backing, nor do they represent current practice on the conduct of reviews.

As we shall see later, many of the organisations submitting written evidence to the House of Commons Select Committee, pressed for the speedy implementation of this section of the 1975 Children Act. However, in November 1980 Sir George Young stated that the government would only press ahead with implementing those sections of the 1975 Act that entailed no net additional costs. The joint working party on the cost of operating the unimplemented provisions of the Children Act reported in October 1980 that :

review regulations will involve local authorities in a substantial amount of additional work and estimated that their additional cost might be in the region of an additional £6 million annually. (Adoption and Fostering, 1981)

One might ask how well the statutory obligations of the local authorities are presently being fulfilled, if the regulation of their conduct would involve so much extra work as to make them financially unacceptable to the government. In delaying the implementation of this section of the 1975 Act the government may well be sacrificing long term benefits for the sake of containing expenditure in the short-term.

A REVIEW OF THE LITERATURE

The existing literature on statutory reviews falls into three categories. First, reports from research projects which have been specifically designed to examine reviews. Second, reports from research projects on other aspects of child care practice, but which include some findings or discussion on reviews. Third, reports or articles which are based upon experience or accumulated knowledge of child care practice, rather than deriving from specially formulated research projects.

Examples of the first category are very limited, and concentrate on two aspects of reviews in child care: the extent to which the regulations are fulfilled, in particular the boarding out regulations; and the degree of participation in the reviews by children and their families.

A major recent survey which monitored social services department compliance with the regulations was carried out by the Social Work Service and published by the DHSS in 1982. This report was very critical of the work of Social Service Departments in fulfilling the Boarding Out Regulations. In referring to the conduct of reviews the report noted that:

> Files were examined in 28 authorities but only in eleven were reviews carried out regularly within the statutory limits ... In some authorities reviews were regarded as a paper exercise or administrative routine and some consisted merely of retyping previous reviews ... Limited use was made of the reviews in planning a child's future ... a very much better standard of work would have been achieved if greater attention had been paid to them as a process for making decisions. (DHSS, 1982)

At present the review process is left to the discretion of individual authorities or even to individual area officers. This has lead to an immense variation in the conduct of reviews, a point made by Stevenson et al in their study of Social Service teams (Stevenson, 1978). At present no comprehensive information is available which details these differing reviewing practices, thereby making any comparative or evaluative study impossible. However in 1983 the Children's Legal Centre undertook a survey - as yet unpublished - of the policies and practices for conducting reviews that had been adopted by all Social Services departments. This survey took the form of a questionnaire plus the collection of written information that had been produced by authorities, such as review forms, guidelines, policy documents.

The Children's Legal Centre is particularly interested in the policies of local authorities with regard to the involve- ment of young people in their reviews and in decision-making in general. This is a topic which is also of immediate con- cern to the Family Rights Group. In 1983 this organisation embarked on an action research project with the aim of working together with two local authorities to devise a system for including parents and children in all reviews, whether held in a Children's Home or an area office. This research is still in its early stages and therefore no findings are available as yet. However, one study on the involvement of children in their reviews was published in 1983, under the title of 'Gizza Say' (Stein & Ellis, 1983). This was the largest research project to have specifically sought the opinions of young people in care and was undertaken by the National Association of Young People in Care with the help of the Centre for Applied Studies at Leeds University. In all, 465 young people were questioned about their attitudes to reviews, how much they were involved and how they thought reviews could be improved. The authors concluded:

> It is clear from our research that there is no national policy or practice about allowing young people to attend their reviews. Some go in for the whole review, some attend for part of the review, some go in to be told the decisions at the end and some young people are never invited to attend at all ... At the present time how young people experience reviews is therefore very much a lottery. (Stein & Ellis, 1983)

Many other studies of various aspects of child care practice have made mention of reviews, without making this the primary focus of the work. Examples of these are the study by Stevenson et al on the work of several social service teams (Stevenson et al, 1978); the study by Lambert and Rowe for the ABAFA of children in care who are in need of permanent substitute families (Rowe and Lambert, 1973); the National Children's Bureau 'Who Cares?' project (Page and Clark, 1977); several research projects set up to monitor the effects of the implementation of the 1975 Children Act (Rowe, Hudleby, Paul and Keane, 1981 and 1984; Adcock, White and Rowlands, 1982 and

14

1983). In general the tone of all these studies has been critical of reviews, mainly in relation to whether, and how, they were conducted. This is well illustrated by the following quotations:

found that 82% of the reports on boarded out children were overdue, and 53% were more than three months overdue; 76% of all reviews were overdue and 50% of them by more than three months. (Stevenson et al, 1978)

In 37% of cases social workers were unable to provide information about whether reviews had been carried out. In 12% only half or less of the required reviews had been done. Social workers could tell us confidently that the full number of reviews had been done in only 35% of cases. (Adcock, White and Rowlands, 1982)

Most, but not all, the study agencies had found it possible to complete the statutory reviews. In the light of this rather encouraging picture on regularity of reviews it seemed somewhat strange that in many cases there should have been such long delays in coming to a decision about a child's need for a substitute family ... even when agencies had carefully devised proforma for reviews these were often completed in such a routine way that they were relatively useless. (Rowe and Lambert, 1973)

The reviews of children every six months is in danger of becoming an administrative procedure rather than real dialogue, and radical rethinking of a child's treatment is militated against by a felt lack of alternatives and insufficient priority being given to preparation for the reviews. (Sayer, Forbes, Newman and Jamison, 1976)

Rowe and Lambert also found that although reviews were held regularly in most of the agencies in their study, they did not necessarily result in action. The authors gave four reasons for this:

This is almost certainly due to (i) failure to set clear priorities, (ii) review decisions which the field work staff do not understand or accept, (iii) team leaders or area directors who were not present at the review, and are not aware of the plan, do not agree with it or do not see what is required and do not allow the social worker time to carry it out properly, (iv) using reviews in a stereo- typed way which complies with regulations but with no real grasp of their potentialities. (Rowe and Lambert, 1973)

While considering research projects that have concerned themselves in some way with statutory reviews mention should be made of three large scale projects on various aspects of

decision making in relation to children in care that have been
financed by the DHSS. These studies, which commenced around
1977, are 'decision making concerning the admission of children
to local authority care', which is being investigated by Jean
Packman at Exeter University; 'social work decision-making and
its effect on the length of time which children spend in care',
which is being researched by David Fruin and Jeni Vernon at
the National Children's Bureau; and the maintenance of links
between children in care and their families which is being
undertaken by the Dartington Research Unit. Although these
projects are nearing completion, no material has as yet been
published. However, it is anticipated that in the course of
conducting these studies information will have been gathered
on reviews and their place in decision-making for children in
care.

Our knowledge base on statutory reviews is not only derived
from academic research but also from accumulated experience
of social work practice and from specific examples of either
good or bad practice that have been shared through publication.

Thus the DHSS 'Guide to Foster Care', which was the outcome
of a DHSS working party on good fostering practice, contains
a chapter on 'reviewing progress'. This contains much sound
advice on how to use reviews to their best advantage, for
example:

> There is general agreement that formal reviewing is
> essential for good case management and that procedures
> for this need to be established and maintained ... In
> addition good administrative and clerical support will be
> necessary ... at the review the family situation, the
> appropriateness of the current placement and plan and the
> efficacy of the social work input will all need to be
> evaluated ... a team or case conference approach has much
> to recommend it ... where the child is not included he
> should ... be given a specific opportunity of expressing
> his opinion prior to the review. (DHSS, 1976)

Similarly, a section on reviews was contained in the report
of the working party established by the National Children's
Bureau 'to consider the care, welfare and education of
children separated from their families for recurrent or long
periods. In particular, to examine the means of planning for
these children so as to promote continuity and quality in
their care, education and welfare'. This report offered
several suggestions for improving the effectiveness of the
review process, some of which are below.

> Regular reviews should be conducted for all children in
> substitute care, ideally when matters have not reached a

crisis point ... provides a means by which continuity of
planning may be achieved. Carefully conducted it ensures
that children do not languish where they are for want of
reconsideration ... regular reviews which from the start
include all interested people will reduce the likelihood
that smouldering differences are pushed out of sight only
to flare up later but unexpectedly ... a review must al-
locate tasks if work is to be done and must set time
limits for their fulfilment and reporting back. (Parker,
1980)

The very serious criticisms of foster care practice contained in the Survey of Boarding Out Regulations (DHSS, 1982)
persuaded the British Association of Social Workers of the need
to give careful consideration to ways of raising the standards
of foster care practice. Having established a working party
to consider the matter BASW produced their 'Guidelines
for Practice in Family Placement' (BASW, 1982). The key
concept of the guidelines is that every child in a placement
has the right to a written agreement which will cover five
basic points concerning that placement. These are: the purpose
of the placement; its duration; the contact with social
workers; contact with natural family; the procedures for
review and termination of the placement. The Guidelines then
elaborate on the purpose of the review, the expected outcomes
from the review and the membership of the review. Hence the
BASW guidleines say that:

every review should produce:
1. a consideration of the events of the last (six)
    months, including developments in the foster home,
    school/work, health, contact with family of origin
    and social work input;
2. An assessment of the present situation in relation to
    the original agreement and/or last review;
3. A plan of work for the next (six) months
4. A long term plan (if appropriate).
(BASW, 1982)

Having considered the process for conducting statutory
reviews on Children in Care in England and Wales, let us
compare this with aspects of child care practice in Scotland
and in the United States of America.

SCOTTISH CHILDREN'S HEARINGS

Statutory reviews in England and Wales and the Children's
Hearings in Scotland differ in context, role and purpose.
Nonetheless they are both key mechanisms for decision-making

in child care cases and hence studies from one situation may be relevant to the other.

One large scale study of Scottish Children's Hearings set out to look at those factors which directly or indirectly influenced the decision-making process. This was published as 'Children Out of Court' by Martin, Fox and Murray (1981). Like the reports on statutory reviews that we have considered, this research was critical of the widespread laxity in the conduct of hearings and listed a great many breaches of the approved procedures. It also found disturbing features in the style of some hearings and, while emphasising the importance of social worker reports, was critical of the information contained in them and of the way in which recommendations were made:

> Recommendations usually have the appearance of having been grafted on at the end of a somewhat discursive description rather than of flowing logically from an incisive review. (Martin, Fox and Murray, 1981).

The study did report that the children's and parent's response to the panels was very positive, they understood what the panels were about, and they saw the panel members and social workers as helpful rather than punitive. Despite their criticisms of failings in the system the authors judged them as 'distinctly successful'. However, it should be noted that this study did not make any evaluation of the effectiveness of the system from the point of view of the subsequent histories of the children who passed through the system. The authors state:

> The reason we were not in a position to pass any final judgement in terms of success or failure was the lack of any agreed criteria by which judgements should be made. If those who designed the system had made an unambiguous statement of its central objectives, it might have been possible to assess empirically with what degree of success this objective had been attained. (Martin, Fox and Murray, 1981)

A very similar situation pertains to the statutory review system in England and Wales as constituted at present. The confusion surrounding the purpose of reviews is one aspect that will be considered when we discuss that topic later in this chapter.

JUDICIAL REVIEWS IN THE USA

The concerns and anxieties expressed about child care practice in Britain are mirrored in the USA where the activities of social work agencies are increasingly the subject of judicial processes (Pierson, 1983). Hence in an attempt to reduce the uncertainty for children in care by more decisive planning, many states in the USA now demand that 'service plans' are made for children in care and furthermore that these plans should be reviewed and evaluated on a regular basis. For example, the state of Texas requires that:

a plan of service shall be developed which specifies each child's need and the way these needs will be met ... The plan shall include the objectives of placement and the estimated length of stay in care. (State of Texas, 1976)

Not only do many states require that these plans be reviewed regularly by the agency, but many now require that they are reviewed and evaluated through the court system. In 1971, Section 392 of the New York Social Services Law was enacted to provide judicial review of all children who had been in foster care continuously for 24 months. (In 1975 this was amended to 18 months.) A study carried out in 1974 of children in care since 1970 was able to compare the subsequent case histories of those children who had been reviewed by the courts and those who had not. It was:

found that the court review appeared to act as a catalyst in getting agencies to examine cases of children in care more carefully, develop plans for them, and take steps to implement such plans. (Festinger, 1975)

The same researcher carried out a later study of children reviewed by the court. She concluded that:

the legislative intent in enacting Section 392 of the Social Services Law was to reduce the number of children who remained in the limbo of foster care, and to obtain permanent homes for as many children as possible, either through discharge to their families or through adoptive placement. The data in this study show that the '392 court reviews' had had a cumulative effect in moving to accomplish this goal.

This study also reported data on the process of the reviews and the implementation of the court orders. Two sets of findings from that study are very relevant to the research on statutory reviews reported in this book. The courts required the social work agencies to submit reports within a certain time. Thirty percent of these reports were not submitted on time, but the courts were very slow to follow this up:

The failure of the court to require reports on time and the failure of the agencies to submit them on time thus

results both in waste of court time and possible postpone-
ment of action on cases. These findings indicate a poor
record by agencies in fulfilling their responsibilities
and by the court in failing to monitor and compel compliance with its orders. (Festinger, 1976)

A monitoring of reports, both in terms of timing and content,
has since been instituted by the court. These findings show
that, as with statutory reviews in this country, a legal
requirement is not of itself sufficient. It is essential that
it is combined with an efficient monitoring and enforcement
procedure.

The second finding which is very pertinent is the assessment
by the researcher of the extent of compliance with the courts'
directives, based on the reports of the social worker to the
courts:

These ratings were based on the activity reported by each
agency without attempting to evaluate the quality of the
work done.

This method of assessment is very comparable to that used in
the study of decision implementation which follows. Festinger
found that the lack of precision in both court orders and the
agency reports led to a high proportion of 'high compliance'
ratings:

a report that mentioned 'working with the mother on
discharge' or 'exploring plans' could mean many things.
Unfortunately, the lack of specificity in many of the
reports forced a relatively lenient view of compliance
... With lenient interpretation, three quarters of the
reports were rated as in high compliance.
(Festinger, 1976)

The problem of effectively evaluating the implementation of
very imprecise directives was one that arose in the present
study, as will be discussed in Chapter 11.

THE PURPOSE OF REVIEWS

From the review of the literature in the last section it can
be seen that thought has been given to how reviews may be used
more effectively. However, the evidence of review practice
suggests that these good intentions do not represent current
reality. Poor practices arise when reviews are accorded a
low priority and hence they lose out when other demands are
more pressing. The low priority accorded to reviews may arise
because of a confusion over their nature and purpose. This
is a point which was highlighted in the editorial of Adoption

and Fostering, No.99, 1980:

> There is no consensus about the object of reviews or the
> form they take or even their importance.

What then is the purpose of reviews? Why is there such confusion over this? Although the statutory basis for conducting
reviews, the 1955 Boarding Out Regulations, still exists, since
that time there have been several changes in the expectations
of reviews. As different aspects of child care practice have
become a dominant concern so the expectations of reviews have
changed, and additional functions have been included alongside
those which reviews already attempted to fulfil. The boarding
out regulations themselves were introduced at a time of great
expansion in the number of foster homes. Hence the primary
purpose in making reviews statutory was supervisory or
managerial: to ensure that Children's Departments at least
kept track of all the children on their books and monitored
standards of care. With the growing evidence in the early
1970's of children 'adrift' in care, reviews were promoted
as a way of monitoring not only the material care that
children receive, but also the decision-making or planning
that social service departments undertake on behalf of their
children. Similarly, the growing trend in consumerism and
self-advocacy in the late 1970's and early 1980's has created
pressure for reviews to be a vehicle for increased client
participation, enabling children and their families to be more
involved in the service that is provided to them. A further
aspect of the current child care debate that has implications
for the review process is that of protecting clients' rights
by monitoring the use of the increasing power of the social
service departments to intervene in the lives of their clients.
We shall briefly consider each of these three developments in
turn.

Reviews and Long Term Planning

Section 59 of the 1975 Children Act (now Section 18 of the
1980 Child Care Act) states that:

> In reaching any decision relating to a child in their
> care, a local authority shall give first consideration to
> the need to safeguard and promote the welfare of the child
> throughout his childhood.

This requirement is now being widely interpreted as a duty
placed upon the local authority to make adequate plans for
their child clients, and reviews are one obvious occasion for
ensuring that this happens. This understanding implies that
the functions of reviews are no longer simply to 'safeguard'
children by monitoring the care they receive, but should

include the more active duty of 'promoting their welfare'.
This purpose of reviews is well recognised in the literature:

> The responsibility of care agencies to make and carry out
> individual plans which meet the needs of children
> entrusted to their care cannot be over-emphasised ... The
> aim of all case reviews will be to agree a plan tailored
> to meet the needs of each individual child and his
> circumstances. (DHSS, 1976)

> The main purpose of a review is to agree a clear plan for
> the future of the child or young person. (BASW, 1982)

Policies to try to relate reviews and long-term planning have
been adopted by several local authorities. Three examples are
mentioned briefly below.

Yvonne Auger discusses the policy and practice of Lewisham
Social Services Department as set out in their 'Guidelines
for the Under Sixes' (Auger, 1980). Reviews play an important part in this. The guidelines say 'until long-term plans
have been made and implemented the cases of all children under
the age of six years will be reviewed every three months'.
These reviews proved to be an essential part of the improvement in planning. 'The pattern of reviews this set up has
served to stress the urgency of the situation to the social
worker.' The undertaking of reviews is not sufficient; they
must be part of the planning process. 'It has been very
important in these reviews for goals to be set from one
review to the next, and for any progress to be real and to be
seen to be made.'

The Social Services Department of Essex County Council
developed what they termed a Child Care Career Planning
(CCCP) section. The first objective of this section was to
ensure:

> that the future of every child in care or about to come
> into care is positively and decisively planned at the
> earliest and most useful time either before or after the
> commencement of the care episode.

This CCCP was seen as an extension of the review system and
not a replacement for it. 'If however the present review
system were to be supervised in accordance with the principles
and practice of CCCP it could be argued that there would be no
need for CCCP.' (Read, 1981).

The London Borough of Wandsworth similarly established a
Children's Advisory Group 'to improve practice in the area of
planning and communicating plans for children in care'. The
research team explain the emergence of this group as follows:

22

Within our own Department the longstanding concern about
the failure of the statutory review system to produce the
necessary plans for children has been given new emphasis
by the closure of some children's homes.

The group concluded that :

the service to children and their families can be improved
only by ensuring that plans which are comprehensible to
all concerned are made at the outset, and that any changes
in those plans are recorded and communicated, together with
the reason for the change. (North Area Research Group,
1981).

Reviews and Participation in Decision-Making

One part of Section 59 of the Children Act, 1975 has already
been quoted. That section continues:

and shall so far as practicable ascertain the wishes and
feelings of the child regarding the decision and give due
consideration to them, having regard to his age and
understanding.

This statement clearly places on local authorities the duty to
consult and involve children in their care in the decision-
making process. The case can therefore be made that if the
functions of reviews are expanded to include a more active
concern with decision-making then they should also serve the
further function of providing a forum for participation by
children and their families. Participation in reviews is
not only canvassed in terms of enhancing the client's rights,
but also for the overall improvement it can bring to child
care practice.

As Parker noted in the National Children's Home Convocation
Lecture in 1971:

Unless and until authorities identify and work with the
network of interests woven around a child, they will not
be able to make reasonable predictions about his future
... The best designed plans will, I am convinced, prove
empty academic exercises and founder unless it is recognised that our interest in deprived children is not the
monopoly of a particular officer, or a special children's
organisation, but is dispersed among many. (Parker, 1971)

A similar point is made by the DHSS in their Guide to Foster
Practice:

A team or case conference approach to reviewing has much
to recommend it, although it may appear to be expensive in
terms of manpower. The membership might include parents,

23

foster parents, the child, residential staff, teacher, medical and nursing personnel. In the long run this may be more economical since it can prevent confusion, provide a better basis for planning and facilitate good working relationships and communication. (DHSS, 1976)

BASW in the 'Guidelines for Practice in Family Placement' are even more explicit in specifying who should attend a review:

The review itself is a formal event at which all concerned with the placement should be present. Membership of the review should consist of:

(a)   the core members who are party to the agreement to the placement. If any of them cannot be present the reason should be given in writing;

(b)   other persons invited because their knowledge or experience is considered to be helpful in this specific situation, or to help put forward the views of the child/young person;

(c)   managers or other specialists, provided that the reviewing team is kept as small as possible but its ability to take decisions is not impaired.

(BASW, 1982)

Reviews and Monitoring

Monitoring, both of the care a child receives while placed in a substitute home, and of the work of the social worker, has always been implicit in the review process. As the statutory responsibilities and formal powers of the social service departments have grown, so has the demand for greater protection of clients' rights. This was a topic that was of concern to the Barclay Committee. They concluded:

Whatever arrangements are made by individual social workers and their organisations for evaluating their work and effectiveness, we are convinced that this will not be sufficient to ensure that all clients' interests are protected and public confidence in social work maintained ... There should be, in our view, an independent inspectorate which would monitor the practice of both social workers and their employing agencies. (Barclay, 1982)

Supporting this recommendation, the second Report of the House of Commons Select Committee on the Social Services, published in the summer of 1982, called for an inspectorate based on the Social Work Service. This suggestion was echoed by the Secretary of State with the publication of a discussion docu-

24

ment in April 1983 (Community Care, 21.4.83).

It is not possible at this point in time to say exactly how this call for greater monitoring and inspection will manifest itself. BASW certainly see a part for their 'Guidelines' which, as we have seen, are based on the concept of written agreements and collective reviews:

> The Barclay Committee has suggested an inspectorate for all social work. Where family placement is concerned, the implementation of the guidelines would clarify the inspector's task and would facilitate the monitoring of practice within the departments. (Hazel, 1982)

Given that statutory reviews are, at present, the primary forum for monitoring child care practices, it is likely that these will figure, in the future, in any increased inspection of the work of the Social Service Departments.

Lest our discussion of the purposes of reviews should appear too speculative, let us finally return to the more official guidelines contained in paragraph 27 of 'A Study of the Boarding out of Children':

> The overall purpose of the review can be summarised as bringing knowledge of the past and present to bear on formulating plans for the child's future. In order to do so it is necessary to bring together and consider all the aspects of parenting shared by the agency, by those caring for the child and by his natural parents. The review must take into account the views of the child and make use of the expertise of other professionals who are involved, for example in his health care and education. The review can also provide an important opportunity for monitoring the work of the social worker who is responsible for ensuring that the child's needs are met. Plans may have to be made within the constraints of resources but they should form the basis of future work with the child, his family and his carers and be related to well-defined time scales. They need consideration both between and at subsequent reviews to ensure that they are amended as appropriate, that there is a commitment to them by those responsible for taking action and that the action required is carried out. (DHSS, 1982)

In this section we have presented many and varied statements about the purposes of reviews. How far do these represent what is actually happening on the ground? Given that many authorities find it difficult to even conduct reviews regularly, is it likely that changes in practice will have kept pace with changes in thinking or in policy? The adoption

of new practices arises from a recognition of the limitations
of the old practices or from benefits to be derived from new
ones. However such an evaluation must be related to objectives. Almost all evaluations of social work practice have
shown that the benefits which the client gains from casework
are greater when the objectives of the casework are explicit
(Goldberg & Connelly, 1981). Similarly any increased benefits
to childcare practice to be derived from changes in the review
process are likely to be greater if the purpose of the review
is made explicit. The perceptions of the functions of a
review therefore would seem to be an important factor and
one which will be explored fully in this research.

This review of the literature relevant to statutory reviews
will be completed by an examination of some of the evidence
submitted to the Select Committee.

EVIDENCE TO THE HOUSE OF COMMONS SELECT COMMITTEE

As noted in Chapter 1, throughout the first half of 1983 the
House of Commons Select Committee on the Social Services held
an enquiry into Children in Care. Evidence was submitted to
the Select Committee from many groups and individuals with an
interest in child care. In many instances these submissions
took the form of substantial documents containing very careful considerations of current and possible future child care
policies. The evidence covered all aspects of child care
policies and practices from a variety of differing perspec-
tives. While our concern is only with one small part of that
practice, it is worth noting that many organisations drew the
attention of the Committee to statutory reviews and in particular urged that Section 3, paragraph 7(1) of the 1975
Children Act (now Section 20 1980 Child Care Act) should be
implemented immediately. The Committee received specific
recommendations on the content of any new regulations covering
the conduct of reviews from many quarters. Although there
were differences of detail the recommendations presented
displayed a high level of consensus. There was broad agreement that :

- regulations on the conduct of reviews should be introduced immediately by the Secretary of State;
- reviews could have a significant part to play in raising
  the standards of planning for children in care;
- the views of children should be presented at reviews.

By way of illustration let us conclude this chapter with
some extracts from the evidence presented to the Committee:

The plan itself needs to be subject to continuous review, not just to secure its implementation (or amendment if necessary), but to monitor the quality of services provided. Section 20 of the Child Care Act 1980 empowers the Secretary of State to make regulations concerning reviews and it is a matter of some concern that consultations with interested organisations have not yet been held. Regulations need to be issued as soon as possible, preferably before the end of 1983.

These regulations should provide for the first review of the child in care to take place within six weeks of admission, and thereafter at not more than four-monthly intervals. Each authority should designate officers to chair reviews who should not have the management responsibility for the case but be of a sufficient seniority to question and challenge those who have.   (BASW, 1983)

Young people of any age have a right to know what is happening to them and every effort should be made to involve them in the decisions made about them; each local authority should draw up a policy about reviews which makes sure that young people fully understand the review process.
Young people should be able to choose people they trust to help them put their point of view and back them up. (NAYPIC, 1983)

The Secretary of State should issue regulations to ensure the function of reviews is to find out how the child is faring, to consider whether care should continue and on that basis to make plans and decisions for the future and to designate responsibility for carrying out these decisions.
Young people over the age of 13 should be entitled to attend the whole of their review.
Reviews should be organised in a place and at a time which is convenient to the child.
(Children's Legal Centre, 1983)

3 Decision-making

INTRODUCTION

While this study is about decision-making in statutory reviews, the relationship between these is complex.

Reviews are not wholly about decision-making - they perform several, sometimes divergent, functions. Similarly, by no means all child-care decision-making takes place in reviews. Indeed, one of the primary purposes of the research was to establish how far reviews are used as a decision-making forum.

This complexity yields three primary needs:

   (i) to develop an understanding of the review process in its entirety;
  (ii) to assess the review as a decision-making forum;
 (iii) to establish the role of reviews in the wider process of child care decision-making.

What these three needs underline, however, is the importance of an understanding of decision-making to any assessment of reviews as a key element in child care practice. This chapter consists of a brief review of relevant literature and from that an identification of issues to be highlighted in the empirical research.

DECISION MAKING AND SOCIAL SERVICE ORGANISATION

Much of the literature on decision-making in the social services relates to policy planning at central government level and at local authority level. This generates discussion of the role of the social worker as an employee of a bureaucratic organisation and hence as the instrument through which policy decisions taken at a higher level are made operational (Hill, 1976). To ensure that these policies are applied consistently and fulfil their intended objectives, the organisation develops a set of rules and procedures in an attempt to regulate the activities of the employees. Discussion in the literature then revolves around the inherent conflict between this bureaucratic model and that of the professional model (Benson, 1973; Davies, 1983). Among other considerations, the professional model envisages members of a recognised profession exercising a high degree of individual autonomy in decision-making, an autonomy that derives from the level of skill and knowledge of the trained professional worker (Hall, 1975). Because of the importance attached to the level of expertise that is expected of a professional, it has been suggested that social workers are more accurately classified as semi-professionals (Etzioni, 1969).

Bureaucratic controls may not only be difficult to apply because of aspirations to professionalism, they may also be weakened by the nature of the social worker's task (Wilding, 1982; Hill, 1972). As Smith (1979) points out, front-line workers usually have considerable freedom to decide their own objectives and methods. They often work independently, away from the departmental office, in a close relationship with their clients. Indeed front-line workers can easily identify with their clients and, like them, may feel the constraints imposed by the Social Service Department as a bureaucratic organisation (Jordan, 1974). The Barclay Committee recognised the difficulties inherent in this three sided relationship:

> We believe that there will always be a degree of tension between practising social workers and the organisation which employs them and the public at large. (Barclay, 1982)

In calling for greater delegation of decision-making to social workers and for formal recognition of their discretion, Barclay argued:

> The challenge for local authorities is to find ways to reconcile controls with a substantial and consistent degree of delegation to social workers. Much of the present tension seems to arise from the fact that social workers have a great deal of de facto discretion and that they need to have it in order to help people properly, yet they work in a structure in which, in theory, they have little or none. (Barclay, 1982)

In his discussion of 'street-level bureaucrats' Lipsky also points to the dilemma arising from the need of a bureaucratic and hierarchical organisation to exercise control over its employees. Yet, as he says:

> bureaucratic accountability is virtually impossible to achieve among lower-level workers who exercise high degrees of discretion, at least where qualitative aspects of their

work are concerned. (Lipsky, 1980)

In the discussion in the previous chapter on the purposes of
reviews, it was suggested that the primary function of reviews
was still a monitoring one. Can we, therefore, describe
statutory reviews as a formal mechanism whereby the front-
line worker must periodically account for the decisions that
he has made through the exercise of his professional autonomy?
Insofar as reviews are used to make plans for the future, are
they a means of establishing a framework for social worker
activity - thereby limiting the discretion of the worker? The
answers are likely to vary in practice. In particular, the
extent of the discretion which a review can exercise over the
operation of a social worker will largely depend on how the
functions of the review are perceived and on the nature of the
decisions taken at reviews. These are both issues to be
examined in some detail in the light of the findings generated
by the research project.

THE DECISION-MAKING PROCESS

So far we have considered decision-making as part of the
policy planning and implementation process and in relation to
its organisational setting. We shall now turn to decision-
making at a casework level and consider the processes whereby
decisions are actually made. This is not a topic which, in
the past, has greatly occupied those in the helping professions. This neglect of the decision-making process stems
largely from an ideological commitment to self-determination,
an ethic whereby the social worker enables the client to
decide for himself, rather than have a course of action
imposed on him by the power and authority of the social
worker. Despite their statutory responsibilities few social
workers are eager to act as 'the coercive social worker'.
Nonetheless, the writings of psychologists and management
scientists on the processes of making decisions are increasingly being seen as relevant to the social services, not only
to administrators and managers, but also to practitioners
(Ashton, 1974).

Perhaps the first thing we should ask of such literature is
what is meant by the term decision-making? Etzioni (1968)
defined it as 'making a conscious choice between two or more
alternatives and selecting the most appropriate means to
achieve the end'.

Simons (1965) took a somewhat broader definition: 'It is
becoming alert to a problem, exploring it and analysing the
different components of the problem and finally deciding on

a course of action'.

Definitions such as these can provide the basis for a model of the decision-making process. The classical model of decision-making is a set of logical steps and has been described by many authors. Lindblom suggests the following formulation.

(1) Faced with a given problem
(2) A rational person first clarifies his goals, values or objectives, and then ranks or otherwise organises them in his mind
(3) He then lists all important possible ways or policies for achieving his goals
(4) And investigates all the important consequences that would follow from each of the alternative policies
(5) At which point he is in a position to compare consequences of each policy with goals
(6) And so choose the policy with consequences most closely matching his goals.

(Lindblom, 1968)

Many modern decision theorists see this rational-economic model of decision-making as being unrepresentative of what actually occurs in practice. Because of limitations on the information that humans can handle and the tasks they can perform simultaneously most decision-makers do not seek for optimal solutions but accept solutions that will solve the problem satisfactorily, although not necessarily in the best possible or ideal way. This concept of limited search and of 'satisficing' was first propounded by Simon (1957) and is generally recognised as a more realistic description of how decision-makers actually perform.

> Decision-makers should not really expect perfection; they should look simply for solutions that meet minimum aspiration levels. (Drezner, 1973)

Nevertheless this classical model can still be used as 'an ideal type' against which decision-making performance can be compared.

Drezner applies such a model of rational decision-making to a particular problem, namely programme planning for a voluntary agency. A more relevant example for our purposes is given by Hardiker and Barker (1981) in 'Theories of Practice in Social Work'. These editors include an example of the use of a model of rational decision-making to evaluate a social worker's assessment in a case of suspected child abuse. The model of decision-making used is similar to that given by Drezner and consists of five distinct stages:

1. Understanding the problem
2. Identification of objectives
3. Identification of alternative solutions
4. Evaluation of alternatives
5. Choice

Each of these five stages are explored through their application to a particular case. These examples show decision-making to be a complex activity, undertaken in a climate of great uncertainty and limited information, yet by structuring the process and being explicit in its operation it is possible to reduce the uncertainty and to clarify the purpose and nature of the task. As Hardiker and Barker conclude:

> In offering this model of rational decision-making as a framework within which to discuss the social worker's actions, we are suggesting that a cognitive approach, identifying logical steps needed to reach a decision, will be a helpful tool in social work practice. (Hardiker & Barker, 1981)

An added dimension to the complexity of decision-making in the social work arena is that of the emotional or subjective involvement of the worker. A social worker needs to be empathetic, to be able to identify with his client's problems, but requires more than hunches or gut reactions when making decisions that have major consequences for their clients. The logical processes inherent in a rational decision-making approach may help to make such emotional responses explicit and thereby raise the level of understanding of all aspects of the situation.

How appropriate is a model of rational decision-making to statutory reviews? The answer to this question depends greatly on the extent to which reviews are perceived as decision-making occasions. It must be remembered that, unlike case conferences, reviews are not called into existence because of the recognition of a particular problem: a review is convened at a particular point in time in order to fulfil a statutory requirement.

> Reviews are artificial devices to replace the continual review of each child's need that takes place within an ordinary family. (Brill, 1976)

While a review may be set in motion through administrative procedure, a problem may be raised during its course which requires a specific decision. Ideally, the review would then proceed along the lines of the classic decision-making model in formulating a solution to that problem. Moreover, it was suggested earlier that many writers believe that reviews have a part to play in improving the standards of long-term planning for children. What is the relationship between this need for a longer-term perspective and the classical model of decision-making.

Advocates of 'planning for permanence' would argue that unless, and until, a long-term plan has been developed and recorded in relation to each child in care, a specific 'problem' does exist. If a long-term plan has not been recorded, all reviews - and in particular early reviews - should start from the position that correcting this shortcoming is the primary goal. A logical exploration of long-term options should result, followed by the selection of a plan. However, this again suggests that reviews can be and should be used to make decisions rather than to ratify or to record them. The prior need is to establish the extent to which statutory reviews are in fact being used to make new decisions or simply to ratify actions or goals which the social worker has already established and furthermore to assess the appropriateness of the review as a mechanism for decision-making of this kind. That is a major aim of this research.

DECISION DIFFERENTIATION

The extent of decision making in reviews is one issue; another is the heterogeneity of child care decisions. Reviews can be seen to encompass several different types of decisions. Sometimes they will be concerned with new or fundamental decisions (for example, to move a child to a new placement) and at other times they will be concerned with more minor or routine decisions (for example, to continue to liaise with the school). This being the case, perhaps an appropriate decision-making model to apply to review situations is what Etzioni (1968) termed 'mixed scanning'. This model employs a combination of the rational and incremental approaches in which fundamental decisions are separated from small decisions, and subject to different decision-making processes. Fundamental decisions are subjected to a broad search process which concentrates on covering alternatives (evaluating and rejecting them until only one remains) but which pays little attention to the details. Minor decisions are given less coverage of alternatives but great attention is paid to the details with the intention of constantly improving, rather than radically changing, the way in which things are done.

This model suggests that different styles of decision-making are appropriate for different types of decision. Applying this to reviews, it further suggests that different patterns for conducting reviews may be appropriate to

33

different situations depending on the particular circumstances of the case. The possibility which arises is that of categorising and differentiating between reviews such that the conduct and organisation of the review may vary according to the purpose to be fulfilled and the nature of the decisions to be taken in each case. This is a possibility that we shall examine further in the report and in the concluding chapter.

Another classification of decisions that is well established in the decision-making literature is that by Simon (1965). Simon divides decisions into two polar types - programmed decisions and non-programmed decisions. This is not a dichotomy but a continuum with highly programmed decisions at one end and highly non-programmed decisions at the other end.

> Decisions are programmed to the extent that they are repetitive and routine, to the extent that a definite procedure has been worked out for handling them so that they don't have to be treated de novo each time they occur.

> Decisions are non-programmed to the extent that they are novel, unstructured and consequential. There is no cut and dried method for handling the problem because it hasn't arisen before, or because its precise nature and structure are elusive or complex or because it is so important that it deserves a custom-tailored treatment. (Simon, 1965)

Simon's distinction between programmed and non-programmed decisions can be seen as building on Etzioni's distinction between fundamental and routine decisions (Etzioni, 1968). This takes the differentiation a stage further in that it can be used to establish criteria for distinguishing between important and less important decisions. In particular, the notion of decisions that are 'consequential' or are so important that they 'deserve a custom-tailored treatment' seem particularly pertinent to child care decision-making. Relating this to a classification of review decisions we could say that decisions which are consequential are likely to be important, that is to say, decisions which have a great impact on the child's life. This method of differentiating decisions will be used to develop a typology of review decisions in Chapter 10.

A further refinement of the term decision-making which seems relevant to review decisions is that proposed by Levin (1972). Levin defines a decision in the following way:

> A decision is a deliberate act that generates commitment on the part of the decision-maker towards an envisaged course

of action of some specificity.

Let us look more closely at the two terms specificity and commitment. Levin uses the term specificity in the following way:

> is simply the property by virtue of which one course of action may be distinguished from another. The higher the specificity of an envisaged action, the more closely will that action be specified.

This definition is too circular to have a great deal of meaning, nonetheless Levin has identified an important issue. This is especially so as the specification of the action appropriate to the decision also establishes the means of judging the implementation of the decision, or its 'ultimate manifestation' as Levin calls it. One of the aims of this research is the assessment of levels of implementation of review decisions. Hence the concept of specificity and its relationship to implementation is one which will be explored in the empirical research.

Levin defines his second concept - commitment - in the following way:

> Commitment towards an intended course of action may be defined as the state of mind arising from the expectation, whether conscious or not, that a penalty - for the decision-maker personally or for the group to which he belongs - will follow from the abandonment of the intention. Commitment is a relative quality, and its strength will be measured by the penalty which is perceived to be associated with substituting another action (or no action at all) for the one intended, before it is implemented. (Levin, 1972)

As we have noted previously, a review is a formal occasion with one function, among others, being that of monitoring casework. If long term planning and the implementation of such plans are crucial to the quality of child care, reviews may have an important part to play in enhancing commitment. At the most basic level the penalties for failing to achieve an objective may be increased, simply by having that objective stated and reviewed. As Levin says 'once his intention is made known to others, he is likely to feel that to alter it without the excuse of new information or a change in external circumstances will lower his standing'. But commitment may be enhanced in other ways . As we have already noted there is a growing demand from many quarters to extend the level of participation in reviews and in child care decision-making. It is certainly possible that decisions made publicly and

35

participatively will carry a heavier penalty for non-implementation and that this in turn will increase the level of commitment to the decision. The level of perceived penalty for failing to implement review decisions may vary with the precise range of functions fulfilled by the review, and hence with the structure and conduct of the review. This then suggests that one variable which may impact upon the level of decision implementation is the way in which the review is structured. It is a factor which we will explore in Chapter 7.

Given the lack of research specifically related to reviews, it is worth turning once again to work conducted on the Children's Hearings in Scotland. In their study of decisions taken at Children's Hearings, Smith and May (1980) were concerned with the processes of decision-making. They did not consider whether the Hearings were conducted according to the rules or established procedures, nor were they interested in the content of the decisions or their eventual outcome. Their specific concern was the nature of decision-making in a situation that was characterised by great uncertainty and ambiguity. The uncertainty and ambiguity of the Children's Hearings arises in part from their multifarious functions (are they for control, for treatment?, etc), in part from inequalities in the perceived status of the participants and their 'evidence', and in part from the lack of rigid rules or procedures. Smith and May concluded that to understand the nature of decision-making in a situation of such uncertainty and ambiguity it is necessary to go beyond the rational model and to see decision-making as a flexible endeavour which is framed to manage uncertainty, to control the situation without an overt display of authority and to obtain consensus between client and professional. Observation of panel discussions led Smith and May to identify six features of the activities that members of the Hearing panel engaged in and which they understood as decision-making. These observed behaviours may represent a considerable departure from the classical model, but they 'are the ways in which purposeful and meaningful activity is maintained in the light of the problems that panel members face' (Smith and May, 1980). In summary,

- the panel saw a decision as 'obvious' and did not look for alternatives
- the outcome was determined by pre-hearing discussions
- the panel passed over major decisions and gave much time to discussion of peripheral matters
- in complex cases, where the panel was unsure how to proceed, they might postpone any action until the next review
- where there were difficult or unmanageable aspects to

36

a case the panel might narrow the focus of discussion,
leaving fundamental problems unresolved
- the panel might spend time in discussing matters which
were outside their power to direct

The approach described here may be peculiar to the particular instance of the Children's Hearings, but the researchers
conclusions alert us to the important relationship between the
style of decision-making and the role and function of the
decision-making forum. The appropriateness of different
styles may vary considerably with the function.

Although there is only a limited amount of research on
decision-making that is of direct relevance to statutory
reviews and their place in child care, some useful leads have
been highlighted in this chapter. For instance the literature does alert us to the importance of

- differentiating between decisions and therefore of the
need to describe decisions;
- relating the style or process of decision-making to
the nature of the decisions;
- the possible impact of public or participative decision
making on the commitment to implement the decision;
- the relationship between the specificity of the
decision and future assessments of its implementation;
- the need to accommodate the style of decision-making
to all the functions of the decision-making forum.

All of these points are taken into account in the design of
the research project which follows. Further consideration
will be given to them in the light of the findings from the
research.

4 The research project: aims and methods

THE RESEARCH AIMS

The starting point for this research was the suggestion from a senior member of a Social Services Department that the review process, particularly for children in residential care, appeared to be characterised by a repetitiousness arising from a failure to implement review decisions. Was this indeed the case? Was there a general lack of activity related to reviews? If this was happening was it true for all children in care, or only those in residential care?

Any attempt to answer these questions raises many others. Before we can effectively evaluate the rates of implementation of decisions we must know something of the nature of the decisions - do they relate to large scale objectives, or specific tasks? Do they include long-term plans, or short-term activities? Decisions which are recorded in a very generalised way - which do not specify goals or actions; which do not include an expected time-scale for implementation - offer very limited criteria against which an evaluation of the implementation can be made. As decisions taken at reviews will not be of a uniform nature, any study of decision-taking and implementation must begin with the development of a typology of decisions whereby review decisions can be classified according to their salient features. Only when this is done is it possible to assess the value of the recorded rate of decision implementation. The development of such a typology was the first aim of this project.

The second main aim of the research was to ascertain what factors contribute to the effective implementation of review decisions. Obviously the nature of the decisions themselves, as discussed above, may be one set of factors which affect implementation. Another main source of variation in the review process was in the organisation of reviews.

Within the particular local authority in which this research
was conducted, statutory reviews on children in residential
care were organised by Care Branch at County Hall. Reviews
on all other children in the care, or under the supervision,
of the local authority were arranged at area office level.
The organisation of these reviews was at the discretion of the
Area Director and in each of three social work areas visited
the review process followed a different pattern. (A description of the research site is contained in Chapter 5.)
This then gave two main sources of organisational variation:

(i)   between reviews conducted in residential
        establishments and those conducted in area offices
(ii)   between reviews conducted in different area
        offices.

As well as organisational or administrative variations,
differences in the style and content of a review may be
reflected in the nature and subsequent implementation of
review decisions. Does the reviewing officer act as a
'chairperson' or is he closely involved in the case? Is the
review discussion mainly retrospective concentrating on
monitoring social worker input, or does the reviewing officer
initiate new approaches or new resource inputs? The
researcher aimed to develop a framework for describing the
style and content of each review and to gather the necessary
data from observation of the reviews.

The style and content of a review will be governed by the
perception that the 'reviewing officer' and other participants have of the function of the review. As we saw in
Chapter 2, there is considerable confusion over the purpose
of a review. Is it seen primarily as a management tool -
'a fail-safe mechanism' - is its main purpose to monitor the
work on a particular case, is it to make decisions, to develop
and record long-term plans? Moreover, is the perception of
the purpose of a review likely to vary depending on the
characteristics of the particular case? Answers to such
questions are necessary in order to establish the context of
our descriptions of review decisions and review processes.
Hence a further aim of the research was to explore the ways
in which members of social service teams viewed the purpose
of reviews. Once all the likely functions of reviews have
been identified, this can be used in several ways:

- to enable the researcher to assess how far each review
  was fulfilling each function
- to ask the social workers which functions they thought
  each review should perform
- to ask the social workers which functions they thought

each review did perform
- to ascertain the opinions of members of the Social
  Services staff (including residential workers and team
  leaders) on the functions of reviews in general.

A fuller appreciation of the perceptions of the review
process would also enable us to assess more accurately the
role that reviews play in decision-making for children in
care.   Decision-making is only a part of the review process,
and the review process is only a part of total decision-
making.   Before the effectiveness of reviews as decision-
making mechanisms can be assessed it is necessary to place
the review within the context of the total decision-making
for children in care.   This then was the final aim of the
research project.

In summary, the aims of this research were:
1. to develop a typology of review decisions
2. to ascertain the level of subsequent implementation
    of review decisions and what factors contribute to
    this
3. to identify the functions of reviews and the way in
    which these are perceived by members of Social
    Service teams
4. to place the review within the context of the total
    decision-making for children in care.

The fulfillment of these aims would generate three distinct
and equally useful outputs:
(i)   a description of the review process detailing what
      happens in a review and further increasing our
      knowledge of 'what social workers do',
(ii) an analysis of the opinions of members of social work
      area teams on the role and importance of reviews,
      particularly in relation to planning for children in
      care,
(iii) the generation and testing of specific hypotheses.

THE HYPOTHESES

Following from the second aim of the project (to ascertain
what factors contribute to the effective implementation of
review decision) two very general hypotheses were established
together with a set of more specific hypotheses.   These
general hypotheses were:

- the rate of implementation of review decisions would be
  related to the way in which the decisions were made

- the rate of implementation of review decisions would be related to the nature of the decisions.

These general hypotheses generated many small scale, but more specific, hypotheses:

(a)   the greater the level of agreement between the participants on the decision, the greater the likelihood of implementation,

(b)   the fuller the participation in the decision-making of those affected by the decision the greater the likelihood of implementation,

(c)   the greater the specificity of the recorded goals the greater the level of implementation,

(d)   the greater the level of specificity of action, and the more responsibility was specifically delegated, the greater likelihood of implementation,

(e)   decisions which included a time-scale for implementation would be more likely to be implemented,

(f)   decisions which had a major impact on the child's life style would be more likely to be implemented.

METHODS

The main unit of analysis to be employed was that of the individual decision. To fulfil all the aims of the research it was necessary to collect data on many aspects of the review process, as well as background information on each case. This was supported by information from the social worker on each case together with their opinions on the reviews. Data was collected in three main ways - by reading case records, by questionnaires, by observation of reviews. Briefly, the steps in the research programme were as follows:

1.   Identification of the children to be included in the sample (for details see chapter 6).

2.   Completion of data sheets on the present and past history of the child's career in care, including the clarity with which the case work objectives and long-term plans were recorded in the case work files.

3.   Observation of the review and the recording of details on:
(a)   the organisation and content of the review, the style of the reviewer, the extent of the discussion of objectives and long-term plans, the functions fulfilled by the review.
(b)   details of the decisions taken, the extent of agreement on these, arrangements for implementation,

the extent of collaboration required, discussion of
resource constraints.

4. The administration of questionnaires to members of
the social work teams on the importance and functions
of reviews, and their level of satisfaction with
them. This information, gathered by questionnaire,
was greatly reinforced by informal discussions with
social workers which also allowed for a measure of
cross checking of data.

5. After each review the social worker was asked to
complete a questionnaire relating specifically to
each individual case. This included questions on the
preparations for each review; the making and
recording of plans for each child and how important
the review was in this process; major decisions that
had been taken on the case in the past year and
where they were taken; any resource constraints on
case work; the extent of the social worker's
agreement with each review decision. Similar
questionnaires were given to residential staff,
though the total number of responses was low.

6. A record was made of all the decisions taken at
every review, i.e. those decisions that were recorded
on the review form and signed by the reviewing
officer. These decisions were then categorised by
the researcher along several dimensions - the level
of impact of the decision, the type of decision (new,
repeat, modified), the specificity of the goals, the
specificity of the action, the timescale, the focus
of the decision, the nature of the resultant social
worker activity. This analysis forms the basis of
our typology of review decisions.

7. Immediately prior to the next review on the child
the researcher reread the case notes (assuming the
case notes had been kept up to date) and recorded
any major changes in the child's life or relations
with the Social Services department.

8. This information was confirmed by attendance at the
subsequent review.

9. Following this second review of each child's case the
social worker, together with the researcher,
recorded the extent and the success of the implementation of the decisions taken at the previous
review, together with the reasons for any non-
implementation.

10. The information collected from these various
exercises was processed by computer.

It will be seen from this brief discussion that the method
employed on this research was basically a quantitative one.
However, the interpretation of the results from this quantitative approach was greatly facilitated by the observations
and opinions gathered informally. In order to complete the
field work as outlined above it was necessary for the researcher to spend considerable time in social work area offices
and to visit many Children's Homes. While maintaining what
was hopefully 'a low profile', this did afford valuable
opportunities to observe an area team at work and to talk to
members of the social work area teams.

It is therefore appropriate to see this project as adopting
several research methods. This triangulation of data gather-
ing is important. By using three different sources -
established case records, structured questionnaires and review
discussions - to collect information on the same topics, the
validity of any one source can be strengthened. Similarly,
the informal knowledge gained by the researcher through
attending social work offices and observing the review process
supported the data that had been gathered, thereby establishing confidence in its analysis.

5 The research site

The research was undertaken in the Social Services Department of a shire county, which for the purposes of this report shall be called Wainshire*. Like most shire counties Wainshire has a mixture of urban and rural environments. It includes one large city with a substantial 'immigrant' population, three medium sized towns, each serving as an industrial centre and as a market town, several smaller towns and an extensive agricultural sector.

It is of interest to compare Wainshire with other local authorities in England and Wales, particularly in terms of demography, numbers of children in care and the resources and facilities available to them through the Social Services.

Table 5.1 below presents demographic statistics for Wainshire; the average for all local authorities in England and Wales and the range covered by individual local authorities.

We can see from this table that local authorities vary greatly in the composition of their populations and therefore in their needs for welfare services. The table also shows Wainshire to be a very average authority in terms of these population characteristics.

Similarly we can compare Wainshire with other local authorities in England and Wales in terms of their Social Services provision, and more specifically in terms of the number of children in the care of the local authority. Table 5.2 shows the figures for Wainshire; the average for

---

* The descriptions given in this chapter of the organisation of Wainshire Social Services Department and three of its area offices applies to the time when the research was conducted, that is 1981 and 1982. Since that time changes have occurred at both area and county level.

44

TABLE 5.1

	Wainshire	Average for all local authorities in England & Wales	Lowest figure for a local authority	Highest figure for a local authority
Total population in local authority	839,400	424,630	116,100 (excluding city of London)	1,468,200
% of population under 5 years	6.3	6.0	3.6	7.4
% of population under 18 years	26.9	25.7	14.4	32.7
% of children in low socio-economic group households	14	16	7	31
% of children in one parent or large families	18	22	13	30

Source: DES Statistical Bulletin 8/82

all local authorities in England and Wales and the range
covered by local authorities.

Table 5.2 shows the great diversity in Social Service
activity within local authorities in England and Wales.
The metropolitan boroughs and the London boroughs in
particular spend considerably more per head on Social Services
than do the shire counties. These figures once again show
that Wainshire is very representative of local authorities
in England and Wales.

WAINSHIRE SOCIAL SERVICES DEPARTMENT

Wainshire Social Services Department is administered from
County Hall. Its responsibilities are carried out through
five branches. These are Research, Development and Training;
Personnel and Coordination; Administration and Finance;
Domiciliary, and Care. This type of organisational structure
approximates to model A as outline in the work of the Brunel
Institue of Organization and Social Studies (Rowbottom et al
1974). This is basically a functional structure in which
the Social Services Department is divided so as to reflect
major areas of activity. A summary of the main advantages
and disadvantages of functional, specialist, or geographical
structures is included in Payne (1979).

Two of the branches of Wainshire Social Services Department
are directly involved with children in care - Domiciliary and
Care branches. Care branch is responsible for all day care
and residential care provided by the Social Services
Department for all ages of the population, including therefore
the provision and management of community homes for children
in care.

The Domiciliary branch is organised into two sections, field
social work and field support services, each headed by an
Assistant Director. The field support services is responsible
for such services as meals on wheels, home-helps, voluntary
services, O.T. The Domiciliary Social Work section is
responsible for all field social work, social work for courts,
in hospitals, emergency and out-of-hours cover, etc. Much of
the work of the Domiciliary Social Work branch is carried out
through the Social Work area offices. Wainshire is divided
into eleven area offices, each headed by an Area Director.

The provision of resources and facilities for children in
care is therefore under the direction of two different branches
of the Social Services Department - the Care branch being

TABLE 5.2

	Wainshire	Average for all local authorities in England & Wales	Lowest figure for a local authority	Highest figure for a local authority
Total gross expenditure on Social Services per head	£34.00	£34.50	£28.0	£139.5
Total number of Social Services field work staff per 1000 population	0.46	0.50	0.27	2.8
Number of children in care per 1000 of the population	7.2	7.8	1.7	24.6
% of children in care who are fostered	52%	46%	27%	77%
% of children in care in community home	40%	38%	14%	58%

Source: DES Statistical Bulletin 8/82; DHSS Children in Care of Local Authorities 1980 CIPFA Local Authority Statistics 1981

responsible for the management of residential care and day
nurseries and the Domiciliary branch for other child care
services. However, the cases of all children in the care or
under the supervision of the local authority are held by a
social worker based in an area office, regardless of where
that child is placed. Field work staff seemed to work closely
with the members of the Care branch, yet many complained of
difficulty in implementing decisions which related to
placements in residential care. These difficulties may be
due to lack of resources, but they may also be emphasised or
felt to be emphasised because of departmental divisions at
County Hall. Similarly communications between residential
staff and field workers may be difficult for many reasons,
but lack of a single line of responsibility may exaggerate
them. This, however, may not be a problem peculiar to
Wainshire. Stevenson et al (1978) came across this in their
study of Social Service Teams:

> However, reading the eight studies of area teams, one is
> struck by the amount of tension and frustration created
> in individual workers when residential places have to
> be found. What emerges is not only to do with shortage,
> though this is in some areas acute, but with the
> difficulties experienced in making contact with those,
> usually 'at HQ' who allocate places ... it would seem
> that more consideration needs to be given to the pro-
> cedures as much as to the actual deficiencies (in
> resources). (Stevenson et al 1978)

The Domiciliary branch of the Social Services Department
had responsibility for all foster care. However, this
responsibility was shared between the staff at County Hall and
those in area offices. Foster parents were regarded as a
'county' resource, rather than an 'area' resource; a child
from any area could be placed anywhere within the county.
The recruiting and assessing of foster parents was in part
shared by both levels, although County Hall were more active
in the former activity, field work staff in the latter. The
Adoption and Fostering Officer, and the Special Placements
Officers based at County Hall played the major part in
matching children to particular foster parents, especially
for long-term or special fostering, but were much less active
in short-term foster placements. The monitoring of foster
care and support of foster parents was almost entirely the
responsibility of field work staff, as were the reviews on
foster children.

The departmental division in responsibility for domiciliary
care and residential care had implications for this research,
in that the review process for children in residential care

48

was different from that for other children. The reviews for children in residential homes were organised from County Hall and were similar for all homes in the authority. Reviews on other children were the responsibility of each Area Director and therefore varied considerably between different social work areas.

SOCIAL WORK AREA OFFICES

The three social work areas employed as research sites encompass the total environmental variety of the shire. Area X is basically a rural area; Area Y is a city area; and Area Z is centred on a medium sized town.

The different environments in which these area offices are situated are reflected in the nature and pressure of requests for social work services and in the resources available to social workers to assist their clients. Table 5.3 compares the three areas in terms of their geography, their population

TABLE 5.3

	AREA X	AREA Y	AREA Z
Geographical type	Widespread rural area	City area with high population density	Large town plus villages
Total population	73,900	64,000	69,100
Caseload/ 1000 population	6.3	12.5	10.6

Source: Wainshire Social Services Department
Quarterly Statistics, June 1982.

and their caseloads. Area X covers a widespread area; it has the largest population, but has the smallest caseload. Area Y on the other hand serves a smaller, high density population, but has a caseload level which is twice that of Area X. The different character of these areas is also reflected in the management and organisation of the area offices.

Area X

This rural area contained two market towns. The social work
was available from two offices, one situated in each of the
towns. Each office was open five days a week, by and large
serving its own locality. The Area Director and the
Administrative Assistant spent three days of the week in the
larger office, two days in the smaller. The social workers,
however, rarely moved between offices, except for staff
meetings. The larger office had two senior social workers
and six social workers, the smaller had one senior social
worker and four social workers. No 'intake' team operated in
this area; new cases were either dealt with on a 'duty' basis
or allocated at weekly meetings. All the social workers
threfore had regularly to perform office duty. If the team
were temporarily reduced through illness or holiday, etc.,
office duty could become a time-consuming part of the job. In
comparison with most inner city areas there were fewer local
facilities that social workers could utilize on behalf of their
clients - e.g. no day nursery was available; there were few
facilities for teenagers either for recreation or for
employment or training purposes.

Both the buildings housing this 'area office' were modern
and spacious with very good secretarial back-up. Indeed,
high standards in administration and casework recording were
expected by the Area Director, and in general were achieved.

Area Y

This was a city area covering a part of the city that
approximated to a quadrant, reaching from the city centre to
the city boundary. Included in the area was a large prewar
council estate with a very high level of deprivation. This
social work area also had two offices, but these operated in a
somewhat different way to those in Area X.

The main office was in the city centre. The Area Director
was assisted by a Deputy Area Director. There was an 'intake'
team and a long-term social work team. This research only
involved members of the long-term team which consisted of two
senior social workers and eight social workers, a social work
assistant, and a specialist fostering social worker.

The other office was a sub-office situated on a large council
estate and was not attended on any sort of regular basis by the
area management team. The sub-office saw itself as operating

a 'patch' team, closely involved in the local community and
somewhat cut off from the rest of the area. As well as a team
leader, there were seven social workers and two social work
assistants. No 'intake' team operated although distinction
was made between short-term and long-term work and caseloads
were biased accordingly. Office duty was a fairly demanding
aspect of the job - indeed, in an attempt to try to control
the bombardment from clients the team leader had decided to
close the office to the public during part of the normal
working week. This team had developed a very thoughtful
approach to the role of the Social Services in their area.
They were developing special skills within the team and
liaisons across the community in an attempt quickly and
accurately to identify the needs of a client and hence to
involve the appropriate skills or resources straight away.

In comparison with the rural area, the social workers in this
city area had more resources, both of their own and from
outside the social services, with which to involve the client
(e.g. day nursery, mothers' groups, active I.T. group, home
start, family service unit, probation and social skills
schemes, various industrial enterprise schemes for unemployed
youths). Other resources which were available on a county
basis but located in the city were more accessible to the
city area than to county areas: for example child guidance,
pediatrician specialists, schools psychological service.
Also, in comparison with the rural area, the job of the
city social workers, including those working on longterm
cases, involved considerably more liaison with other welfare
or service agencies, e.g. housing department, social security,
electricity, gas.

The accommodation for the two offices in this area was of a
very poor standard. The sub-office was situated in a council
house; eleven people worked in four tiny rooms upstairs. There
was inadequate room to interview clients; one secretary shared
a room with a social worker; there was no administrative
officer and constant movement to and from the main office of
stationery, letters, files, people. The main office was
equally overcrowded. All the long-term team, including the
seniors, were in one office with no spare rooms for consultation with the senior. On several occasions when carrying
out the reviews, the senior social worker and the researcher
had to carry all the files and necessary paper work outside
the building, along the street and into another building,
where the use of a spare office had been begged. Again there
seemed to be inadequate secretarial support to keep case
records, reports and review forms up to date, although the
obvious gaps in case work recording cannot all be blamed on

51

overstretched typing facilities.

Area Z

The bulk of the population served by this area office lived
in one large industrial town; the remainder lived in a number
of nearby villages. All the Social Services were housed
together in one modern office near the centre of the town.
The social work staff was divided into an intake team and a
long-term team. No members of the intake team were involved
in this research. The long-term team comprised two senior
social workers and eight social workers. As in Area Y the
members of the long-term team helped with office duty, but
this was a much less significant task than for those workers
in Area X or the sub-office of Area Y where no intake team
operated. Secretarial support did not appear to present any
problems in this office but - unlike the other offices visited
- the reviews were spread throughout the year. This office,
more than the others, showed a continuity of staff - indeed
several children had had the same social worker for sixteen
years. The Social Services Department had good resources,
and had excellent relationships with voluntary agencies and
organisations in the town.

  Without wishing to place too much emphasis upon it, one way
of establishing how these different offices picture themselves, is to compare their job advertisements:

  Area X
  To complete social work team serving this area. If you
  want ...
  * a manageable generic caseload
  * regular supervision and opportunities for professional
    development
  * membership of mainly qualified teams covering mixed
    urban/rural areas presenting a variety of problems
  * time, facilities and encouragement to do the job
    properly
  * no standby duties

  Area Y Sub-Office
  HELPING LOCAL RESIDENTS HELP THEMSELVES!
  A skilled worker is required to join this experienced and
  enterprising 'patch' team, situated on a postwar Council
  Estate with the highest concentration of deprivation in
  'the city'. The team has built a reputation for providing
  a service which attempts to meet local needs most
  appropriately and effectively. This includes - information
  and counselling; contract work; behaviour modification;
  family therapy; women's group work and I.T; liaison with

local residents and agencies and community development; family placements. There is short and long-term involvement and co-working. The team is well integrated and supportive, offering excellent opportunities for the expression of particular abilities and interests and further training. A post for the experienced, looking for new challenges or a newly qualified seeking rapid professional development.

Area Z

Qualified, enthusiastic person required to join the long-term team in which child care policy is being examined. (I.T.,foster parent applicants groups, G.P. liaisons and mothers' group now established). Case loads have child care bias, but room exists for individual interest to be followed. Regular supervision given high priority, and a case load weighting system exists, although this is currently subject to area review.

COMPARATIVE STATISTISTICS FOR THE SOCIAL WORK AREAS

Comparative case loads

Having looked at the different environments in which these three social work area offices are located, we now turn to look in more detail at the caseloads held by each office and the proportion of child care cases within the total caseload.

Throughout this local authority not only are children who are in the care of the authority subject to statutory review, but all children under supervision orders or on the 'at risk' register are also included in the review process. Cases in all these categories are referred to as 'statutory' cases.

The use of this very broad definition of 'statutory' cases seems to be a widespread practice, although this does not necessarily mean that other authorities included all their 'statutory' cases in the review programme. The researchers on the DHSS study of Social Services Teams certainly found a broad use of the term statutory:

We asked all our respondents what work was considered to have priority. The answer hardly varied - it was 'statutory' work. This phrase is vague and imprecise. When we probed we found that it referred to children in care, or to work with families and children which either came from the courts or might lead to some public investigation by a court or inquiry if 'things went wrong'. 'Statutory' did not, amongst our respondents, mean all or only work required by statute. (Parsloe, 1981)

Table 5.4 below shows comparative statistics on the caseloads of each of the three areas, including statistics on the
total caseload, those dealing with families and those subject
to review. This shows that a very much higher proportion of
all cases in area Y are child care cases which are subject to

TABLE 5.4

	AREA X	AREA Y	AREA Z
Total case load	504	726	802
Number of cases dealing with children and families	186	561	420
Number of cases subject to review	121	489	226
As a % of total caseload	24.0%	67.4%	28.2%

Source: Wainshire Social Services Department Quarterly
Statistics, June 1981

six-monthly review. One can see, therefore, that in this
area the completion of reviews must be a sizeable task.
Indeed the number and proportion of all cases which are
reviewed must have major implications for the organisation of
the review process.

Comparative legal status/placements

The composition of the 'review cases' in terms of placement and
legal status within the three areas is shown in Table 5.5.

Although we have already shown that the child care statistics
for Wainshire are very representative of England and Wales as
a whole, and in particular of the shire counties, we can see
from the statistics in Table 5.5 that different areas within
the authority do produce different patterns of child care
cases. This is in part due to demographic and environmental
factors and in part due to different emphasis or policies
pursued by each area director, within the overall policy of
the Social Services Department. For instance, although Area Y
has a large number of children on the 'at risk' register
(116 compared with 55 in Area X and 73 in Area Z) a much
smaller proportion of these cases have no other statutory
order. Review discussions showed that in Area Y social

54

TABLE 5.5

	AREA X	AREA Y	AREA Z
Total number of review cases	121	489	226
% of those boarded out	25.6	20.0	19.5
% in residential care	19.8	28.0	13.7
% home on trial	12.4	10.8	6.2
% other	2.5	1.6	1.8
% on supervision order	13.2	24.7	31.0
% on at risk register (this includes only those children who are not included elsewhere - many children may be on 'at risk' and be in care)	26.4	14.7	27.9
% of review cases who are 'in care' (i.e. first four categories)	60.3	60.5	41.2

workers, under the direction of the area director, were much less likely to remove a child from the register or to leave an 'at risk' child at home with no statutory supervision than was the case in other areas - no doubt as a result of a relatively recent child abuse inquiry in that area. Area Y also has a much higher percentage of children in residential care than other areas. This was not an issue which the research examined, but several factors probably contributed to this. Area Y is an area of high social deprivation, particularly in the large council estate. Here the problems of delinquency meant that many of the children coming into care were teenagers and therefore less likely to be immediately fostered. As in many social work offices, social work practice in this area was undergoing change, and staff did express the view that they were still dealing with the backlog of consequences of past social work decisions, when a higher proportion of children were placed in residential care. Whatever the reason for the high proportion of children in residential care in this area, the concern generated by this and the desire for change had lead to the first and, at the time of the research, the only appointment of a fostering specialist within an area office.

SUMMARY

This chapter has provided a background to the research by describing the demography and environment of the county and three of its social work areas.

The population characteristics of the shire and the activities of Social Services department both point to Wainshire as a very representative county and local authority area.

The three social work areas within Wainshire in which the research was conducted are very different in their environments and hence in their social work activities. This can be seen in particular in their case-load levels and in the number of child care cases within those caseloads.

6 The research sample

In the last chapter we looked in general terms at the wider
research context; in this one we shall look more closely at
the populations and the samples drawn from them.

THE SELECTION OF CASES

The required date for the review of a child's case is related
to the date of his reception into care. In theory reviews
will be spread over the year, with no significance attached
to reviews which fall in any particular part of the year. To
fulfil the original plan of covering 50% sample of reviews,
one would, therefore, include all the reviews that fall due
within any three-month period. However, in none of the
research areas were cases reviewed continuously, according to
the chronological reception into care. Therefore the method
of sample selection was chosen to take account of the
particular way in which the review process was organised in
each area. Also, because this research was designed to follow
cases through at least two reviews, it was decided at the
outset to exclude very short-term cases, and cases on the
point of closure. Consequently, in those areas where an
'intake team' was in operation the population was assumed to
be those cases held by members of the long-term team.

In Area X, all reviews were conducted within a two-week
period and as this area had a smaller caseload, it was
possible to include in the research all those cases which were
reviewed.

In Area Y, reviews were conducted over a two-months' period,
so rather than cover the cases of all social workers over half
the review period, it was decided to cover the cases of half
the social workers over the whole period when reviews were
taking place, giving approximately a 50% sample of long-term
cases.

In Area Z, reviews were held every week, each time covering
the caseload of one social worker. Here the sample was

selected by including all the cases of the long-term social
workers which were reviewed within a three-month time span,
again giving a sample of approximately 50% of long-term cases.

The reviews of children in residential care were organised
by Care branch at County Hall, under different arrangements
from the reviews conducted in area offices. Therefore the
criteria for including children in residential care in the
research sample had to be somewhat different. Having selected the social workers from each area who were to participate
in the research, as explained above, children in residential
care who were on the case loads of these social workers were
also included in the sample. Because of clashes in the
review timetables it was not possible for the researcher to
attend all the reviews on children in residential care.
Consequently, the number of residential reviews at which
research material was collected is smaller than that indicated
by the sampling framework.

A COMPARISON OF THE SAMPLE CASES WITH THE TOTAL CASELOAD OF
EACH AREA

Each social work area office completes quarterly statistical
returns for the Research and Development branch of the Wainshire Social Services Department, as well as annual returns
for the DHSS. These figures can be used as a point of
comparison against which to test the representativeness of the
sample. However, the cases covered in the statistical returns
differ from those included in the sample in four ways:

   (i)   The sample was drawn only from cases held by the long
          term team, excluding cases held by 'intake', where an
          intake team was in operation.
  (ii)   The research criteria excluded short-term cases and
          those on the point of closure - these will be included
          in the statistical returns.
 (iii)   Some children on the 'at risk' register appear twice
          in the statistical returns, e.g. on a Supervision
          Order and 'at risk'. The 'at risk' category is only
          used in the research for those children under no
          other order. Corrections to take account of this
          have been made from information received from the
          administrative officer in each area. As this was
          collected at a different time to the statistical
          returns they are subject to error.
  (iv)   The caseloads of social workers - and the status of
          children on those caseloads - are very fluid, so the
          statistical return information will only be accurate
          at the time it is collected.

So long as these caveats are borne in mind it is useful to compare the sample included in the research with the full caseloads of the areas as shown by the statistical returns of June 1981. This comparison is made in two ways: (1) the placement of the children and (2) their legal status.

(1)   The Placement of Children

Table 6.1 shows the pattern of the placement of children in the three areas combined, and in each area separately. It shows the percentages taken from the statistical returns of June 1981, and those in the sample. Children who are 'home on trial' are children who are subject to a Care Order and therefore 'in care', but living at home. The last category in this table, At Home, refers to those children who are under a supervision order, or whose names are on the 'at risk' register and who are living at home. These children are not 'in care', but in this authority were regarded as 'statutory' cases for review purposes.

   The figures show that the sample is under-represented in children in residential care and over-represented in children in foster care. However, given the comparatively large numbers of cases included in the total sample, these differences should not be of great importance: each type of case is represented by an adequate number of cases in the sample. Whether the sample or the statistical returns is the more accurate reflection of the actual caseloads at the time that the sample was taken is impossible to say.

(2)   Comparisons of Legal Status Categories

Statistical returns of the legal status of each child in the care of a local authority (by area) are made to the DHSS annually. The figures used in Table 6.2 were taken on 31.3.82. These only include children actually in the care of the local authority and exclude children on supervision orders or 'at risk'. The number of children in these categories in March 1982 has been collected from the Administrative Officer in the area.

   This table shows a wide variation between the three areas in the proportion of children in each category, according to the statistical returns. Part of this variation could be due to different methods of collection or to accounting error. The rest must be explained by the differing environments of areas and the pursuit of different child care policies.

TABLE 6.1

PLACEMENT	AREAS X & Y & Z		AREA X		AREA Y		AREA Z	
	% from statistical returns	% of sample	% from statistical returns	% of sample	% from statistical returns	% of sample	% from statistical returns	% of sample
Boarded out	20.7	33.2	25.6	28.1	20.0	35.9	19.5	34.5
Residential	23.0	16.6	19.8	17.0	28.0	17.7	13.7	11.5
Home on trial	9.8	9.2	12.4	9.0	10.8	11.6	6.2	4.6
At home	44.8	41.7	40.0	46.0	39.4	34.3	58.9	49.4
	100.0	100.0	100.0	100.0	100.0	100.0	100.0	100.0

TABLE 6.2

Legal Status	AREAS X & Y & Z		AREA X		AREA Y		AREA Z	
	Statistical returns %	Sample %	Statistical returns %	Sample %	Statistical returns %	Sample %	Statistical returns %	Sample %
Section I* (1948)	15.2	8.8	24.0	7.9	8.6	8.3	15.2	11.5
Section II* (1948)	6.6	11.4	5.6	12.3	3.4	8.3	6.6	16.1
Care Orders & Interim Care Orders	25.5	36.7	25.6	30.7	48.2	45.3	25.5	24.1
Supervision Orders & Matrimonial Supervision Orders	29.2	20.5	17.6	19.3	26.3	16.0	29.2	29.8
'at risk'	23.3	21.5	27.2	28.1	13.5	18.8	23.3	18.4
Ward of court	0	1.0	0	1.8	0	3.3	0	0

* (Now Section II and Section III of 1980 Child Care Act)

Comparison of the statistical returns with the sample shows
a much larger proportion of children in the sample who have
been subject to assumption of parental rights resolutions. We
feel that much of the explanation for this lies in accounting
error. Children who are subject to a parental rights resolu-
tion come into care voluntarily in the first place. The actual
procedure which moves a child from one category to the other
can be lengthy and notification of the change-over may not be
immediately passed to the administrative officer.

The low representation in the sample from Area Y of children
on supervision orders is most likely to have arisen because
reviews on these children are a non-statutory obligation and
therefore likely to be given a low priority. For instance,
some of these cases, while being held officially by the local
authority, were on the caseload of the Family Service Unit,
which carried out all necessary social work intervention,
and therefore these may have been missed at review sessions.

SUMMARY

The sample selected for this research comprised all cases
reviewed in Area X in one six-month period, and approximately
50% of the cases reviewed by the long-term teams in Area Y and
Area Z.

A comparison of the composition of the caseloads of these
areas, in terms of the placement of children and their legal
status, reveals considerable variation between the areas. A
comparison of the total caseloads with those in the sample
also shows some differences. These differences are not felt to
be of any great importance, given the large number of cases
included in the sample and the caveats with which the
statistical return data have to be surrounded.

7 The review process

In this chapter we shall look at the organisation and structure
of reviews. The review process can be divided into three
stages: the preparation for the review, the arrangements and
conduct of the review, and the follow-up to the review. We
shall look at each of these aspects in turn. However, before
doing so, it may be best to give a brief overall description
of the conduct of reviews in this particular authority. As
was pointed out earlier, there were two main divisions in the
organisation of reviews: between residential and non-
residential reviews and between reviews carried out in different area offices. Thus the research covers four different
arrangements for conducting reviews.

Residential Reviews

The reviews in residential homes were organised by Care branch
staff at County Hall. For most community homes this meant that
two dates were set aside each year for holding statutory
reviews. On these dates the statutory reviews would be held
on all the children living in the home at that time (individual reviews could be held at other times, if necessary).

In two community homes in the city with a high proportion of
teenagers, one date each month was set aside for reviews and
in the two O and A centres one morning each week was set aside
for reviews or case conferences. Because of the nature of O
and A establishments case reviews were held much more
frequently than was statutorily required.

Two specialist residential establishments in the county
arranged their own reviews. The consensus of opinion voiced
by many workers was that these establishments gave statutory
reviews an exceedingly low priority. At times this resulted
in a failure to conduct reviews when statutorily required;
failure to complete the necessary review forms, failure to use
reviews to develop long-term plans and a failure to implement
them. This criticism is related specifically to statutory

reviews and not necessarily to the quality of their work with the children, or relations with social workers.

The policy in most community homes of holding all the reviews in a batch once every six months, meant that up to twelve (most commonly seven to ten) reviews are held on one day, chaired by the same reviewing officer and with the officer-in-charge in attendance at each. This may have the advantage of focusing the mind on reviews, but one must seriously question if the cases reviewed at the end of the day received as much attention as those at the beginning. However, most reviews will involve different personnel and this can help ensure that each session has some elements of a fresh start.

Area X

In this area all cases were reviewed within a two-week period. For a fortnight, twice a year, therefore, the Area Director would concentrate, almost exclusively, on reviewing cases. Each social worker in turn would present all their 'reviewable' cases. However, the case-loads in this area were comparatively small: no more than ten cases were presented at any one session. This policy of concentrating the reviews, together with the stress that the Area Director placed on administrative efficiency, made every one in the area team very 'review conscious' - thereby ensuring that reviews were given a high priority. Given this attitude, the arrangement for conducting reviews 'enbloc', did ensure that all cases were reviewed on time. Even if a case were transferred from one social worker to another it would not fall outside the six-monthly review period. However, this arrangement may also raise problems of tight scheduling, which may not be flexible enough to cope with difficult cases. For instance, in one review it became apparent that there were very complex issues at stake, of which the Area Director had not been aware. This needed detailed and lengthy consideration - much more than was allowed for in a review. The Area Director remarked 'a review is not the place to bring this up' - because it was a serious matter which needed immediate attention. However, this suggests that the role of reviews is seen primarily as monitoring past work and transferring information rather than casework planning - a topic which will be discussed in chapter 9.

This arrangement meant that the Area Director was chairing over eighty child care cases in two weeks. Did this level of concentration have any implications for the quality and incisiveness of his performance as a reviewing officer? One senior social worker did suggest that content, in terms of in-depth or insightful probing, may be sacrificed in order to achieve administrative efficiency, although Table 7.4 shows that the average length of reviews in this area was longer than in the other areas.

Area Y

As pointed out in Chapter 5, this area had a very high proportion of 'reviewable' cases. Because of this a two-tier review system was in operation. Cases were initially reviewed and review forms completed by the senior social worker; the up-to-date files and reviews were then passed to the Area Director or Deputy Area Director for scrutiny, and a second, much less detailed, review session was arranged.

Because of the total number of cases to be reviewed, the two-tier system, and the fairly complex nature of many of the cases, the whole review process was a time-consuming exercise. The aim was to complete all reviews within a two-three month period. Dates for the review with the senior and the Area Director were arranged about a month in advance. However, these dates were often rearranged because of illness, holidays and case 'blow-ups', so the whole process often stretched over a longer time than anticipated. From reading the case files and records of case loads it was apparent that some cases did escape review. These were most often: cases on supervision orders, especially matrimonial supervision orders; private fostering which were not statutorily required to be reviewed, but which departmental policy suggested should be reviewed; cases held by the Family Service Unit; or cases in which there had been a change of social worker. The frequency of changes of review dates also meant that more than six months often elapsed between reviews.

Area Z

In this area the Area Director held reviewing sessions on Tuesday mornings, reviewing all the cases of one social worker on each occasion. Each social worker would have two such sessions in a year. The timetable for these reviews was set well in advance and the dates rarely changed. The sessions with one social worker could last from four to six hours, depending on the number of reviewable cases. Although this batch reviewing could present problems of decreasing freshness as the session wore on, at least the occasion only occurred once a week and did not therefore present problems of cumulative lack of freshness. The social workers in this area kept detailed caseload lists which were regularly updated, so it was rare for a case to miss a review - although a change

in social worker could well mean an extension of the interval
between reviews. The senior social workers were not included
in review sessions, and did not appear to be greatly involved
in the preparation for the review. The exception to this was
that seniors regularly attended residential reviews with their
social worker, more so than was the case in the other areas.

Having briefly described the four different arrangements for
conducting reviews we shall now look at the review process in
three stages. The preparation for the reviews; the arrangement and conduct of the reviews; the follow-up to the reviews.

THE PREPARATION FOR REVIEWS

Under this general heading we shall look at two sets of tasks:

    (i) The use of review forms
    (ii) Other preparatory tasks undertaken by the social worker.

The review forms

(a) Layout of the forms. Three different review forms were
used throughout Wainshire: one for residential reviews; one
for children who are boarded out; and one for all other casework reviews. The headings used in each of these forms were
varied to suit the particular purposes.

Social workers were asked how satisfied they were with the
forms and if there were any changes they would like to see
made. Satisfaction was lowest with the residential review
forms; over one-third of respondents were fairly or very
dissatisfied, compared with one-fifth who were dissatisfied
with forms used in area office reviews. Over 70% of social
workers and residential staff wanted some changes made. These
changes ranged from specific details to more fundamental
changes such as asking children or parents to complete part of
the form. In relation to residential reviews the most
frequently cited change was to reduce the section giving
details concerning reception into care to allow for much
fuller discussion of changes since the last review, particularly in relation to the family situation. Indeed, several
homes abandoned or supplemented the prescribed form and
produced their own review reports. Several residential staff
also asked for information on fieldworker involvement (e.g.
the number of visits) to be included. None of the review
forms included the decisions from the last review, nor did any
of them ask about the objectives of the casework, or the long-
term plans for the child. Inclusion of such material could
increase the extent to which the review is used for critical

evaluation of the objectives as well as the details of case-work.

(b) The completion of review forms. This was a task that was fundamental to all reviews and was basically the same for all social workers, regardless of the organisation of the review or the characteristic of the cases. However, completion of residential review forms differed from the completion of area office forms in several ways:

- for the social workers they were one-off reviews and scattered through the year, hence allowing for great concentration on a single case. However, residential review forms were not seen by the Area Director, which appeared to reduce their significance to the social worker, as they were often completed with minimal attention.
- the social worker only completed one part of the residential form, the residential staff prepared one part and the reviewing officer completed the final section at the review.
- the social worker had the responsibility of collating all these and ensuring that copies were sent to everyone who kept records on the child. Social workers seem to feel that this task symbolised the administrative clumsiness of the department which may explain why it was not always carried out as well as one would expect. Indeed, at one residential review no-one – neither the social worker, residential staff, nor chairman – had a copy of the previous review and as a new social worker was involved no-one seemed to know much about the case.

The design and completion of the review form is an example of standardisation, over the county, of one aspect of the review process. This is one sort of standardisation, that could be expected if that part of the 1975 Children Act on regulating reviews was eventually implemented. Does it increase the quality of the review? It does to some degree, in that at least once every six months the basic details on a case must be noted. Could this be increased further? Almost certainly yes, by the inclusion of questions on the objectives and long-term plans for each child. However, from observation and discussion it was clear that the gains from completion of a review form varied dramatically, largely dependent on the style of the individual social worker. Some social workers took the opportunity presented by reviews consciously to stand back from their work on a case and systematically to reappraise it, reaffirming or modifying their objectives and methods. Other social workers simply copied not only the details of a case but their comments on behaviour, etc. from the previous review form, hence adding or gaining nothing from the process. The gains from completing the review form are likely to be diminished by the 'batch' review system. If a social worker who is working under pressure has ten or twenty reviews to complete in a limited time then she cannot afford to take too long on each. Neither is the social worker able to overcome this problem by starting the reviews well in advance of the set date, as in many cases the information, or conclusions, get out of date very quickly. It was not a rare occurrence for a social worker to have to start again from scratch having completed a review form in good time only to find the circumstances of the case suddenly and drastically altered.

When the reviews of several social workers are concentrated together this can create great pressure on the secretarial staff. This was particularly a problem in Area Y and often social workers had to retrieve hand-written reviews from the secretaries' 'in-tray'. The team leader in the sub-office in Area Y tried to overcome the necessity to complete review forms hurriedly by giving all his staff three working days at home, away from the pressures and constant demands of the office, so they could gain the most value from completion of their review forms.

The value to be gained from well prepared review forms will be greater if these forms are then used both in the review discussion and in supervision when considering casework plans and priorities. Reviewing Officers used the review forms at most reviews but in a variety of ways. For instance they could be the main source of information on a case with which they were not familiar; indeed merely reading and signing the review form with minimal discussion did constitute the total review on several occasions. At other times reviewers asked the social workers to report verbally on progress and made scant use of the material on the form.

In Area Y which operated a two-tier system, the seniors used their review sessions to check on both the details and comprehensiveness of the form and ensured these were accurate and adequate before being passed on to the Area Director. In all areas examples were found of inconsistencies between the details on the case record and those on the review form, which were often repeated at consecutive reviews.

(c) Recording review decisions. The last section on each form concerned future plans. The recordings made in this section are what we have subsequently used as 'review decisions'. It perhaps appears odd that we should consider review decisions in the section on 'preparation for the review', but in fact many social workers come to the review with their decisions already prepared and recorded. There was a range of practices of formulating and recording review decisions not all of which are appropriate to this section on preparation. However, for ease of comparison, it is best to discuss these together.

In residential reviews the final section was seen as arising from the review discussion. In most Children's Homes the chairman formulated and recorded these towards the end of the review. One must seriously doubt whether a chairman hurriedly composing plans for the future and recording them on the review form while the rest of the group continue the discussion is the most effective way of ensuring comprehensive decision-making. In a group discussion it would be more appropriate for someone other than the chairman to keep a record.

In the case of area office reviews, practice varied from area to area. In Area X social workers discussed their decisions with their senior prior to the review and came with these prepared. Modification or addition to these by the Area Director was always possible, but in practice this was not a frequent occurrence.

In Area Y there was no single pattern. The practice adopted reflected the preference of the individual social worker and each seemed to be quite unaware of the practices of others in their team.

In Area Z the Area Director formulated all the decisions during each review. The style of this particular reviewer was first to record summaries of the present situation. These sometimes lead on to a 'decision' in terms of action to be taken, sometimes not. This was a useful guide to the reviewer as to whether he had covered all necessary points, but it tended to combine and thereby confuse information with decisions. This may reduce the impact of the decision-making aspect of the reviews and increase the informational and monitoring aspects.

Tasks undertaken in preparation for reviews

Social workers were asked which of the following list of eight tasks they undertook specifically as preparation for a review. Table 7.1 shows the percentage response rate for all reviews combined, for residential reviews, for all area office reviews and office reviews for each of the three areas.

TABLE 7.1

	All reviews n = 246	Residential reviews n = 37	All area office reviews n = 209	Area reviews in X n = 72	Area reviews in Y n = 85	Area reviews in Z n = 52
1. Updating case records	59.3	37.8	63.2	52.3	83.5	44.2
2. Talks with child	26.0	43.2	23.0	22.2	27.1	17.3
3. Talks with child's family	35.4	43.2	34.0	36.1	32.9	32.7
4. Contact with school	28.0	24.3	28.7	36.1	24.7	25.0
5. Contact with Health Visitor	7.7	0	9.1	15.3	4.7	7.7
6. Talk with Foster Parents	29.3	5.4	33.5	27.8	43.5	25.0
7. Talk with residential staff	12.2	78.4	0	0	0	0
8. Talk with colleagues	54.1	62.2	52.6	63.9	40.0	57.7

Obviously not all tasks are appropriate for all cases. For instance 'talks with the foster parents' will only be relevant to children who are boarded out. Social workers talked with foster parents in 68% of cases where a child was fostered, although answers to a subsequent question show that less than half the foster parents were told about the forthcoming review. Table 7.1 shows differences between preparations for residential reviews, area reviews and also between the different areas. Social workers do less administrative work for residential reviews but do talk more to the children and their families. This could be related to the age of the child as the mean age of children in residential care is higher than that of children who are fostered or on the 'at risk' register. Also children in residential homes are very aware that 'it is the reviews' and are therefore able to prompt social workers to talk to them about this.

Comparisons between the areas show that social workers from Area Y spend more time immediately prior to a review in updating their records. From our observation it would seem that this is not because they wish to achieve a higher standard at the review but because their records were not as well kept in the intervening six months. Failure to make case recordings on a continuous basis increases the pressure prior to a review session, which must decrease the opportunity to use the preparation for a review constructively. The greater consultation with Health Visitors in Area X is probably due to the larger proportion of children who are 'at risk' and a greater reliance on the health visitors due to the lack of a day nursery. Social workers in Area Z are least likely to talk specifically about the review with the child, the family, or the foster family. Indeed, social workers in Area Z carry out fewer tasks as specific preparation for the review. This could be because they visit homes and liaise with other professionals as a matter of course. Or it could be because the greater spread of reviews in Area Z prevents the office from becoming so 'review conscious'.

THE ARRANGEMENT AND CONDUCT OF REVIEWS

In this section we shall move from the brief overall description given earlier to more detailed information on the review process in each area. We shall use responses to three questions to raise several important issues on the conduct of reviews. These three questions are:

   (i)   What was the interval since the last review?
  (ii)   How long did the review last?
 (iii)   Who attended the review?

(i)   What was the interval since the last review?

This research was not designed specifically to test how far
the statutory regulations were being adhered to in terms of
the interval between reviews. However, we do have some
information on this. As we noted in Chapter 2, much of the
criticism of reviews points to a basic failing to carry out
reviews on time. The national study carried out by the Social
Work Service during 1979/80, and published by the DHSS in
1982, showed that out of twenty-eight authorities examined only
eleven regularly conducted reviews within the statutory time
limits (DHSS, 1982). Three areas in Wainshire (different from
those used in this research), were included in the Social
Work Service study and their unpublished report relating to
these areas suggested that the organisation of reviews
ensured that most were held within the statutory limits.
Wainshire is almost certainly not a typical authority in this
respect. As we have noted previously the organisation of
reviews is at the discretion of the area director, but the
lead given by senior management from County Hall on the
expected standards and priorities undoubtedly has an impact
at area level. The introduction of a social worker manual is
an example of an attempt by senior management to influence the
work of social workers at area office level. These manuals
were issued to all social workers in Wainshire and set out the
procedures to be followed in particular situations. The entry
on reviews included the basis of statutory requirements, the
timing of reviews and the particular points that should receive
consideration in appropriate instances.

At each review attended, note was taken of the date of the
previous review. Table 7.2 shows the results for all reviews
combined, for residential reviews, for all area office reviews,
and for reviews in each area office.

These results show that the vast majority (93.4%) of reviews
in residential homes were carried out within six months and
the remainder within eight months. Overall, 81.7% of reviews
held in area offices were within six months of the previous
one; however, 4.6% of these reviews were more than three months
late. There are differences between the areas: Area X has only
3% of reviews over the six months, compared to 28.4% of reviews
in Area Y and 16% in Area Z. This confirms our earlier
description of Area X as being administratively efficient, and
of Area Y as struggling to cope with a large number of reviews
with poor secretarial back-up. The delays in Area Z were
caused by changes of staff and illness.

Statutory reviews are part of the long-standing boarding-out
regulations; are the cases of children in foster care more

72

TABLE 7.2

TIME SINCE LAST REVIEW	All reviews n =292	Residential reviews n = 61	All area office reviews n = 231	Area X reviews n = 73	Area Y reviews n = 100	Area Z reviews n = 58
Less than 3 months	8.3	18.0[1]	8.4	9.1	12.5[2]	0
3 months to 6 months	75.7	75.4	73.3	87.9	58.3	84.0
7 months to 8 months	11.9	6.5	13.1	1.5	20.8	14.0
9 months to 12 months	1.9	0	2.3	1.5	4.2	0
12 months +	1.9	0	2.3	0	4.2	2.0

1. The larger proportion in this category is due to the inclusion of reviews from O and A centres.
2. The larger proportion in this category in Area Y is because several reviews from the last round were very late in being held.

likely to be reviewed on time? Table 7.3 shows the interval
since the last review for children who are fostered, at home
on trial, at home under supervision and in residential care.

TABLE 7.3

Placement	Interval since the previous review		
	0 - 6 months	7 - 8 months	9+ months
Fostered	77.7	17.4	4.8
At home	84.2	11.8	3.9
Home on Trial	88.9	3.7	7.4
Residential	93.4	6.5	0

There is no statistically significant difference (at a 5%
confidence level) in the timing of reviews for children in
these four categories.

As was noted earlier this research was not specifically
designed to test how far the regulations were being adhered
to. Data was collected on a sample of cases presented for
review. Therefore, cases which had fallen through the review
net could not, by definition, be included in the research. We
do not know how many cases this involved. However, observation and quick comparison of caseloads with cases reviewed
suggested that it was unlikely for cases to be missed in Areas
X and Z, but that this did occur occasionally in Area Y.

(ii) How long did the review last?

In this section we are reporting on the length of the actual
review, including the reading of the review form, the
discussion and recording of decisions. This however does not
take account of any prior activities such as listed in Table
7.1 nor the completion of the review form.

Table 7.4 shows the distribution of the length of the reviews
for all reviews, for residential reviews, for all area office
reviews and for reviews in each area office. These results
point to the striking differences in reviews in residential
homes and those in area offices. In residential homes no
review lasted less than eleven minutes and over 20% lasted
more than fifty minutes. In contrast, in area reviews 7%
lasted less than five minutes and 50% were no more than ten
minutes in length. There were differences between the areas
in the time that was spent on reviews. Reviews in Area X were

TABLE 7.4

LENGTH OF REVIEW	All reviews	Residential reviews	All area office reviews	Area X reviews	Area Y reviews	Area Z reviews
	n = 292	n = 62	n = 231	n = 73	n = 100	n = 58
Less than 5 minutes	5.5	0	7.0	1.4	8.0	12.1
5 – 10 minutes	33.8	0	42.6	34.3	54.0	32.8
11 – 15 minutes	15.7	3.4	19.1	17.8	19.0	20.7
16 – 20 minutes	11.0	0	13.9	20.5	8.0	15.5
21 – 30 minutes	16.1	33.5	11.6	13.9	8.0	15.5
31 – 40 minutes	7.2	21.8	3.3	8.4	1.0	1.7
41 – 50 minutes	5.8	19.6	2.1	4.2	1.0	1.7
51 – 60 minutes	4.1	19.6	0	0	0	0
60+	0.3	1.6	0	0	0	0

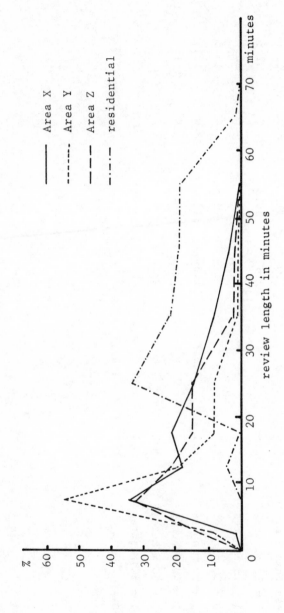

FIGURE 7.1

longest and Area Y shortest. This could be explained, in part, by the thoroughness with which the review forms were studied in Area X and in part by the two tier system in Area Y - where reviews were held by senior social workers who should have greater knowledge of case details. However, the differences between the areas are insignificant in comparison with the difference between residential and area reviews, see Figure 7.1.

Among area reviews, were children in care given longer reviews than those being supervised?

There was no statistically significant difference in the length of area reviews for children who were fostered or home on trial or at home under supervision. Table 7.5 shows that more than half the reviews on children in foster care lasted ten minutes or less.

TABLE 7.5

Length of Review	Children in foster care	Children home on trial	Children living at home under supervision
10 minutes or less	51.9%	57.2%	42.9%
11-20 minutes	26.4%	39.3%	39.6%
20-30 minutes	15.1%	3.6%	11.0%
30+	6.6%	0	6.6%

The length of time a review lasts is not in itself an indicator of the value of a review, but presumably it does say something about what the participants hope to gain from a review and therefore how they perceive the purpose and importance of the review.

Another example of decision-making for children in care which we discussed in Chapters 2 and 3 is the Scottish Childrens Hearings. Although these Hearings are not initiated for the same reasons as statutory reviews in England and Wales, they offer a useful comparison of decision-making processes. Martin and Murray found in their study of children's hearings that on average the hearings lasted forty minutes. This is very similar to the length of residential reviews included in this study, but much longer than the average length of reviews held in area offices (Martin and Murray, 1976).

Another established forum for decision-making on children is child abuse case conferences. Evidence was collected by the

NSPCC on 777 conferences on child abuse cases. This shows that 42% of the conferences lasted up to one hour, that 52% lasted between one and two hours and 5% lasted even longer than two hours (Castle, 1976). These conferences are therefore much longer than those reported by Martin and Murray and the residential reviews included in this investigation.

However, in their study of case conferences on suspected child abuse cases, Hallet and Stevenson (1980) point to the many complaints that are expressed especially by doctors, about the length of these meetings. Child abuse case conferences serve somewhat different functions from those of statutory reviews but the large number of participants, from different professions probably contributes to the length of the conference, and to the probability that beyond a certain length conferences yield diminishing returns. This is a point that should be considered in any proposals to extend the membership of reviews.

(iii)   Who attends reviews?

The difference in the character of residential reviews and area office reviews is again strikingly demonstrated by the attendance at the review, as is shown in Table 7.6.

TABLE 7.6

Number present at review	Area Office reviews n = 231	Residential reviews n = 61
2	93.5	0
3-4	6.5	8.2
5-8	0	52.5
9-11	0	36.1
12+	0	3.2
	100%	100%

In only one area review was anyone other than the reviewer, social worker or senior social worker present. This was the inclusion of foster parents at one review in Area X.

In contrast residential reviews are much more akin to case conferences in that outsiders with knowledge of the child are invited to attend. These were most frequently representatives of the school, although employers, health visitors, doctors and police also attended at least one of the reviews studied. The natural parents were present at four reviews and the child

78

was present at six reviews.

The question of 'who attends a review' raises three very different issues. The first is the wider participation in decision-making of those affected by the decisions, the second is who should act as chairman or reviewing officer and the third is the organisational impact of a broadening of reviews.

Participation in Reviews. This topic was considered in general terms in Chapter 2, where note was made of the relevant section of the 1975 Act. This reads as follows:

> In reaching any decision relating to a child in their care, a local authority shall, so far as practicable, ascertain the wishes and feelings of the child regarding the decision and give due consideration to them, having regard to his age and understanding.

To what extent did the social workers covered by this research fulfil this duty by including children in their reviews? In only 2.1% of all the reviews studied were children included. All of these were children in residential homes, so in 9.8% of residential reviews were children included. On these occasions the children or young people were usually only brought in for part of the review; on only one occasion did a young person attend throughout the review. On several other occasions the young person had been given the option to attend but had declined to do so.

It is of course possible for children to express their wishes or feelings without actually attending the review. However the evidence from this research suggests that this was not happening. Social workers were asked if the child had been informed that a review was taking place; only 19.9% of all replies were affirmative, although 56% of children in residential care had been so informed. Also, as reported earlier, for only 26% of all reviews, or 43.3% of residential reviews, did social workers report 'talking to the child' as part of the preparation for the review. This survey, therefore, suggests that most children in care in Wainshire are not included in their reviews, nor are they informed that a review is taking place. Although a greater proportion of children in residential care are involved in reviews, the numbers are still very small. Instances of the involvement of the natural parents or the foster parents are even less frequent (Sinclair, 1982). It had been hoped to test the hypothesis that decisions made when the child is present are more likely to be implemented than those taken when the child is not present. However, the small number of cases at which the child was present makes the testing of this hypothesis impossible.

The reviewing officer. In all the reviews conducted in these area offices, the role of the reviewing officer was taken by either the Area Director or by the senior social worker; in the residential reviews this task was performed by the representative from Care Branch who had responsibility for the establishment, or occasionally by the Area Director from the area in which the Home was situated. If reviews are to offer a truly critical evaluation of a case then a reviewing officer who is independent from the case, and is not in a position of line-management responsibility may be better able to undertake this task.

As we saw in Chapter 2, in the United States of America the desire for an independent reviewing officer has been met through the use of judicial reviews. This is not a system that has many advocates in this country. However, in their evidence to the select committee BASW recommended that:

> Each authority should designate officers to chair reviews who should not have line management responsibility for the case but be of sufficient seniority to question and challenge those who have." (BASW, 1983)

Would the use of independent chairmen have made any significant differences to the reviews studied in this research? The chairman of the review can influence the style and the conduct of the review, as we shall discuss in the next chapter. A chairman who does not have line management responsibility for a case is likely to have less knowledge of the case, and therefore a review could consist largely of information exchange. However this is less likely to happen if the reasons for holding a review are clearly articulated. However it must be recognized that the adoption of independent reviewing officers for all the reviews undertaken in this authority would have major organisational implications.

The organisational implications. The opinion expressed by almost all organisation interested in promoting good child care practice is that the review process should be broadened to include those most closely affected, the child and his family. This opinion was also voiced by many of the social workers included in this survey. Such a move would have little impact on the basic structure of residential reviews; it would totally alter the ways in which reviews on other children were carried out in Wainshire.

As has been pointed out earlier, a very large number of cases were due to be reviewed every six months, because of the Wainshire policy of including in the review process not only

children in its care, but also children on supervision orders
and on the at-risk register. In all areas reviews were conducted in 'batches' covering one social worker's caseload at
one session. This form of organisation is only practicable
if the review time per case is comparatively short. As the
previous section has shown many reviews held in area offices
are of a very short duration. If every review were to be
broadened, allowing for greater participation by the child
and his family and other interested professionals, or if the
reviewing officer was independent and not involved in line
management of the case, then a structure more akin to a case
conference would have to be adopted. This would certainly
imply that more time and resources would need to be committed
to reviews. The joint working party on the costing of the
implementation of the 1975 Children Act attempted to estimate
the additional costs involved in adopting regulations on the
conduct of reviews. On the assumption that these regulations
would require reviews to be more thorough and involve a wider
group of participants, the working party estimated "that the
effect of review regulations might be to require local
authorities to spend about <u>six more hours on each review</u> than
at present" (DHSS L.A.A. October 1980).

If this estimate were applied to Area Y, in which almost
500 cases were reviewed, twice a year, then the estimated
additional work load would be a phenominal 6000 hours a year!

The actual <u>net</u> addition would depend on the existing standards of review, those functions being carried out elsewhere
at present that this different review style could fulfil, and
the improvement in overall standards of child care practice
that followed from changes in the review structure. Nonetheless to change the existing pattern of area office reviews to
one which involved a greater range of personnel undoubtedly
would have a major impact on the work in the area offices in
Wainshire. An alternative approach may be to <u>prioritise</u>
reviews so that a different review structure was adopted
depending on certain criteria (such as length of time in care,
legal status, placement, etc.). In Chapter 3 we introduced
Etzioni's concept of 'mixed scanning' as a method of
differentiating decision-making. Etzioni introduces this
concept to suggest that different decision-making processes
may be employed for different types of decisions. If this is
applied to the review situation one can see different review
processes being appropriate for decision-making related to
different situations. For instance a large-scale case conference style of review, where all options are explored fully,
may be appropriate as a first review, or where there has been
major changes in the child's circumstances. A smaller review
may be appropriate when a case has been reviewed thoroughly in

the recent past and no changes have occurred since.

THE FOLLOW UP TO THE REVIEW

If reviews are to have real significance, the outcome of their
deliberations must be fed back into casework plans. Was this
done as a formalised process, in an ad hoc way, or possibly
not at all? No direct quantitative measures were taken which
would answer these questions, but we can make some generalised
comments on the basis of observations and discussions. It
would appear that limited use is made of the review forms after
the review. Indeed one gained the impression that generally
they were looked at again only when preparing for the next
review.

A social worker or senior social worker may use a supervision
session as a means of ensuring that reviews are adequately
followed up. However, this did not appear to occur consistently in all of the areas studied. Supervision sessions were
usually limited to a few cases which were particularly active.
Nonetheless, despite the lack of any formal follow-up
procedure, the majority of decisions were implemented.
Interestingly, during the research on implementation, social
workers expressed surprise on several occasions when reminded
of a decision that had been reached at the previous review
and which subsequently had been implemented. This suggests
that social workers carry in their heads a 'framework of
action' for each case and that they use this framework rather
than written records to guide them in their day-to-day
activities. Such an approach has limitations - it makes it
difficult for other workers who become involved in a case and
it reduces the capacity for effective monitoring and supervision. These limitations emphasise the need for both aims and
casework plans to be properly recorded and for these records
to be employed in regular reassessment.

Furthermore, when social workers were asked to give their
objectives on a case, without reference to their records, they
found it much easier to list necessary short-term or continuing activities than long-term goals. This suggests that
the practice of 'carrying cases in your head' gives emphasis
to the short-term at the expense of the long-term, and to
means at the expense of ends.

SUMMARY

In this chapter we have considered the arrangements for conducting reviews in four settings; residential homes throughout
Wainshire and in each of three area offices.

Each of the three area offices were different from each
other in all aspects considered, but these differences were
minor, particularly in comparison to the differences between
'residential reviews' and 'area office' reviews in general.

Some of these differences are summarised below:

RESIDENTIAL REVIEWS	AREA OFFICE REVIEWS
Reviews were arranged by Care branch from County Hall.	Reviews were arranged by each Area Director.
Reviews were often arranged as a 'batch' within the home but were 'one-offs' for the social worker.	'Batch' reviews for each social worker's caseload – although the total review process was spread differently in each area.
Review forms were completed by the social worker, the Residential Officer-in-charge and the Reviewing Officer; they were not seen by Area Director; the decisions were recorded at the end of the review by the Reviewing Officer.	Forms were completed by the social worker; all seen by the Area Director; decisions were recorded in different ways in each office.
Preparation for the review - updating of case records was not an important task. - discussions with the child were held in 43% of cases.	- updating of records was an important task. - discussion with the child were held in only 23% of cases.
93.4% of reviews held within six months of the previous review.	81% of reviews held within six months of previous review.
No review was less than 11 minutes in length; 20% were more than 50 minutes in length.	50% of reviews lasted ten minutes or less.
The average attendance was eight people, ranging from four to fifteen.	In only one case was anyone other than the social worker, senior social worker or Area Director present.

RESIDENTIAL REVIEWS	AREA OFFICE REVIEWS
Children were included in 9.8% of reviews.	No children or their families were included in any reviews.
56% of children were informed that a review was taking place.	Only 11% of children were informed that a review was taking place.

As well as these differences between residential reviews and area office reviews the findings from this chapter highlight three issues:

- the potential for improvement in the use of the review form.
- the lack of family participation in reviews.
- the organisational implications of expanding area office reviews.

None of the review forms used in Wainshire included the decisions from the last review, nor did any ask questions about the objectives of the casework or the long-term plans for the child. Inclusion of such material could increase the extent to which the review is used for critical evaluation of the objectives as well as the details of casework. This may also increase the use of review forms subsequent to the review which could reduce the dangers that arise when social workers are too reliant on caseplans that they carry in their heads.

In the social work areas studied in this research participation by the children in their reviews was extremely limited.

Although residential reviews did involve several different professional groups, the child was included in less than one tenth of the reviews. In area office reviews no children were involved. Indeed only once, when foster parents attended, did area reviews include anyone other than the social worker, senior social worker or the Area Director. Furthermore, only a small minority of children had been informed that their review was taking place.

Not only are area office reviews limited in their participation, many are of a very short duration, suggesting limited discussion. However, because of the large number of cases which are reviewed in these areas, any change from the existing pattern would have major implications for the organisation of work. Indeed it would seem to be impossible to restructure all the reviews at present undertaken along the lines suggested by BASW, among others, in their evidence to the select committee. If area office reviews were to be broadened both in scope and participation then some system of prioritising may be necessary.

8 The content and style of reviews

THE CONTENT OF THE REVIEW

In this chapter we shall develop further the descriptions of reviews by considering the content of the reviews and the style generated by the reviewing officer. The content of each review discussion is particular to that child and his circumstances at the time, and hence any generalisation or meaningful measurement of the content is not easy. Nonetheless, the content of all the reviews was analysed by several complementary methods. The findings from this analysis are summarised in two ways:

(a) by using a 'check list' of possible discussion topics;
(b) by highlighting the extent of discussion on the objectives of each case and the means and the time-scale to achieve these objectives.

(a) Check list of possible discussion topics

Our pilot study suggested seven broad headings which would be likely to encompass the range of the topics discussed. These were: medicals, the present placement, the behaviour of the child, the progress of the child, family relations, finance, and social worker contact. A record was made each time a topic was discussed to some purpose, during a review. The results can be seen in Table 8.1. However, a reviewing officer may have noted details from a review form, e.g. that a medical had been conducted, and if this was satisfactory he may not have raised the issue in discussion. In so far as this was happening, it suggests that reviews were being used for information exchange.

Obviously the topics discussed will vary with the type of case. For instance, medicals are specified in the boarding-out regulations and are therefore more appropriate for children who are fostered. Similarly finance will be important in terms of boarding-out allowances especially for requests for special payments, and for families with children 'at risk', where an area officer may use his discretion to approve

TABLE 8.1

DISCUSSION TOPICS	All reviews	Residential reviews	All area office reviews	Area X reviews	Area Y reviews	Area Z reviews
Medicals	16.8%	11.5%	18.2%	4.1%	9.0%	51.7%
Present placement	28.4	31.5	27.7	31.5	29.0	20.7
Behaviour of child	53.4	72.1	48.5	56.2	50.0	36.2
Progress of child	51.0	78.1	43.7	28.8	34.0	79.3
Family relations	51.4	73.8	45.5	56.2	44.0	34.5
Finance	11.0	3.3	13.0	12.3	5.0	27.5
Social worker contact	11.0	1.6	13.4	12.3	20.0	3.6

expenditure for 'preventative work'.

Table 8.1 shows some interesting differences in the content
of reviews. Residential reviews are more often concerned with
the child's behaviour and progress, but much less interested
in finance or social worker contact. The differences between
the different areas in part reflect the distribution of types
of cases in each area and in part reflects the particular
concern of the reviewing officer. In Areas X and Z all cases
were reviewed by the Area Director, in Area Y the cases
were reviewed by three different senior social workers,
which explains the greater emphasis in this area on social
worker contact - senior social workers are more likely to
adopt elements of a supervisory role.

(b) Objectives and Means

In Chapters 1 and 2 references were made to the growing
concern over the lack of planning for children in care. One
of the questions which this research addresses is the role of
reviews in improving planning. It is important therefore to
ascertain how far reviews were being used as an occasion to
either develop or reassess or reaffirm long-term plans. Each
review was assessed by the researcher in three ways, using
different sets of alternative descriptions. The first set
related to the discussion of long-term case objectives. The
next two considered each review as a decision-making exercise
and the researcher assessed which of five alternatives gave
the best overall description of the discussion and of the
decisions.

TABLE 8.2

Long-term Objectives	All area reviews	Residential reviews
Assumed and not discussed again	25.2%	6.6%
Reaffirmed	19.1	26.2
Re-examined	26.0	52.5
None of these	29.6	14.8
	100.0%	100.0%

Table 8.2 summarises the way in which long-term objectives
were covered in reviews in area offices and in residential
homes. Long-term objectives were discussed in considerably
less than half the reviews in area offices, although in a

quarter there was an unspoken assumption about what these objectives were. However, information gained from reading the case records shows that in only a quarter of all cases were long-term objectives recorded in the case files. This is interesting in the light of the case being promoted by BASW and others for written agreements to be made which set out the objectives of the social services when taking a child into its care or under its supervision. Discussion on long-term objectives occurred more frequently in residential reviews. A placement in residential care is often regarded as temporary or as a stepping stone to a more permanent placement or to independent living and hence one would expect to find a greater emphasis on the longer term in residential reviews.

The five alternative ways of describing, overall, both the discussions and the decisions taken at reviews are shown in Table 8.3.

TABLE 8.3

	DISCUSSIONS		DECISIONS	
	Area Reviews	Residential Reviews	Area Reviews	Residential Reviews
1. A holding operation because of expected changes	3.9	3.3	7.4	9.8
2. Development of long-term plans without specific decisions about means	4.8	6.6	3.1	4.9
3. Development of long-term plans including short-term goals	17.5	62.3	14.0	50.8
4. Short-term tasks with no reference to long-term goals	25.3	16.4	27.5	19.7
5. Maintenance of the status quo	48.5	11.5	48.0	14.8
	100%	100%	100%	100%

This again points to a limited emphasis on long-term plans
in the content of area reviews, in contrast with a major
emphasis on this in residential reviews. Almost half of all
area reviews were best described as 'maintaining the status
quo'. In these cases the review is most likely to be fulfilling a monitoring function, rather than a decision-
making one - a point which shall be developed in the next
chapter. The general picture of review discussions drawn
from this summary of their content is of an emphasis on
retrospective analysis rather than prospective planning. A
picture which can be compared to 'the position of a driver
travelling forward but steering himself by the view his
driving mirror affords of what has already happened'.
(Sheldon, 1982).

STYLE OF THE REVIEW

As with the previous section on content, the style of the
review is closely related to its functions and this aspect
will be discussed later. What we are concerned with now is
the extent to which the reviewing officer can determine the
character of the review, either by the seriousness with
which he treats the occasion or by the nature of his chairmanship. It was apparent that individual social workers
varied in what they put into reviews and in what they felt
they got out of them. However, this variation was to some
extent limited by the standards established by the reviewing
officer. Variations of these standards were in turn limited
by the declared expectations of senior management at County
Hall. Both the Domiciliary and Care branches of the Social
Services Department appeared to give reviews a fairly high
priority, at least in terms of ensuring that they were completed on time. It is possible that this was reinforced by
the inclusion of parts of Wainshire in the DHSS study on
boarding-out regulations carried out in 1979/80 - as no doubt
the study reported here also influenced the review process in
those areas which were researched. Senior management had also
approved a section on Reviews for inclusion in the procedures
manual held by all social workers. This set out the deri-
vations of the requirement to review and questions that should
be considered. One must say however, that this represented
the ideal rather than the actual picture of review discussions.

Even within the climate which the Social Services Department
attempted to establish, the Area Directors still have considerable scope to influence the general attitude to reviews
in their area, as have Care Branch officers in the Homes they
supervise. One important way of doing this is through the

organisation of the reviews and the time spent on them, as reported in the last chapter.

Other actions of the Area Director help to establish the priority or seriousness with which reviews are treated. For instance, does the reviewing officer accept telephone calls or other interruptions during a review? If he makes it clear that there are to be no interruptions, except in absolute emergencies, this establishes the reviews as having a high priority. Similarly, a high priority will be established if only unavoidable absences or emergencies are seen as acceptable reasons for postponing a review. Using these criteria, all the reviewing officers could be said to take their reviews seriously - in particular the Area Director in Area X.

NATURE OF THE CHAIRMANSHIP

Each reviewing officer will have his own way of chairing a review. Does this produce important differences in the style of the review? Twelve phrases were used to describe possible reviewing styles. These were:- has prior knowledge of the case; systematic; acts largely as chairman; explores new approaches; asks about the child's wishes; probes social worker input; accepting of the status quo; reflects policy downwards; emphasises accountability; accepts the social workers assessment; accepting of resource constraints; explores new resource alternatives.

Although several different chairmen were involved in both area and residential reviews there are still some points of generalised comparison to be made between these two types of review. In area reviews the reviewers took a more directive line; were more systematic in their questioning; had greater knowledge of the case; probed social work input much more fully; emphasised the need for accountability. In contrast, the reviewing officers in residential reviews were more likely to act as chairman, facilitate discussion rather than initiate it - although they were more likely to explore new approaches or new resource inputs; more likely to ask about the child's wishes; express less concern about accountability, and the need to reflect the policy of senior management. In comparing reviewing styles between the different areas we must remember that in Area Y several different people acted as reviewing officer, most often this was a senior social worker so we could expect the style of these reviews to be somewhat different. In comparison to an area director a senior social worker would have more knowledge of the cases and may have recently held supervision sessions with the

social worker at which these were discussed. Nevertheless,
in summary, the main differences are:

    AREA Y   Less systematic questioning
              More acceptance of the social worker's assessment
              Less probing
              Less exploration of new approaches

    AREA Z   More concern about the child's wishes
              Less acceptance of the status quo
              More exploration of new resources

    Area X   Very systematic
              Fuller probing of social work input

SUMMARY

From this analysis of the content of reviews it can be seen
that the discussion in residential reviews tended to cover
different topics from those in area offices and also to
examine these topics with a more purposive and longer term
perspective. Indeed, in a high proportion of area reviews
the content of the discussion was confined to a summary of
events of the past few months and anticipation of the next few
months.

   However, any meaninful discussion of the content of a review
must be related to the review process, as was discussed in
the previous chapter, and also to the functions of the review
- which is the subject of the next chapter.

9 The function of reviews

Earlier, in Chapter 2 attention was drawn to the confusion which surrounds the purpose of reviews. It was suggested that there have been changes in the perceived purposes of reviews, in that many writers assume that the range of functions appropriate to, or expected from, a review has broadened. However much of this discussion has been based on what is considered as desirable, even possible, for a review to achieve; it has not been based on knowledge of the way in which reviews are presently being used.

Furthermore, the appropriateness of any proposed structure for conducting reviews, or any guidelines on their content or decision-making style is likely to depend on their explicit functions.

For these reasons it is important to have a full understanding of all the functions actually fulfilled by reviews and also of the opinions of members of the reviews on the functions that they feel they should fulfil.

In this chapter we shall examine the range of possible functions of a review and assess the importance of these in practice.

WHAT ARE THE FUNCTIONS OF REVIEWS?

Through discussion with members of social service teams a check list was developed which contained ten possible functions of reviews.

1. ADMINISTRATION   – A check on case records and the details on the review forms

2. MONITORING   – Monitoring the implementation of earlier decisions

3. SUPERVISORY   – A check on the work input of the social worker

4. DECISION-MAKING   – To make new decisions

5. INFORMATIONAL (i)   – To inform Area Director and/or senior of work input and problems and hence safeguard the social worker

6. INFORMATIONAL (ii)   – To co-ordinate information on case/resources from different personnel

7. SPECIFICITY   – To make earlier decisions more specific and to identify sub-goals

8. DEVELOPMENTAL   – Staff training and development

9. REASSESSMENT   – To reassess systematically the appropriateness of earlier decisions

10. LONG-TERM PLANNING   – To develop and record long-term case plans

Each of these functions is self-explanatory and the respondents had no difficulty in understanding them, with the possible exception of No.5, INFORMATION (i). This was intended to cover those instances where the social worker purposefully initiated the information transfer, but it seems that this was interpreted by the respondents to include any transfer of information to the Area Director or senior, regardless of its initiator or purpose. It also followed from this that function 6, INFORMATION (ii), was used most often in reference to residential reviews where others than the Area Director or senior were present, and hence information exchange was very relevant.

The check list was used in several different ways to gather information about the functions of reviews. The format in which the different questions were asked are listed below, with the number of respondents.

(a) A questionnaire to members of the Social Services area teams (31) and senior residential staff (11) asking:
    (i) Consider the list of possible functions of a review. Tick any you feel a review ought to fulfil.
    (ii) Which in the one most important function in residential reviews; in area office reviews?
    (iii) How satisfied are you with the review procedure in relation to those functions which you have ticked below?

(b) A questionnaire to social workers after the completion of individual reviews (246) which asked 'which functions should have been, and were, the main concern of this review (please tick up to maximum of five different functions)'.

(c) Data collected by the researcher when attending reviews as an observer (292) which addressed the following question: how far does the review appear to be carrying out the functions listed?

The first point to make about reviews is that they are multi-functional. The complexity of the purposes that reviews are expected to fulfil is seen by the number of functions ticked by each respondent. Members of Social Services area teams ticked an average of 6.5 functions while residential staff saw reviews as even more diverse in their purpose and ticked an average of eight functions.

WHICH FUNCTIONS ARE MOST IMPORTANT?

If we rank the 'functions that a review ought to fulfil' by the number of times it was ticked by respondents, we see four clear priorities:

1. Monitoring
2. Long-term planning
3. Making new decisions
4. Reassessment of previous decisions

Two functions were clearly regarded as least important:

9. Supervisory
10. Staff training and development

In the middle ground a number were bunched closely together:

5. Administrative check
6. Information (i)
7. Making decisions more specific
8. Information (ii)

The only real difference in the ranking produced by residential officers and field social workers was the relative importance the latter attributed to reviews as an administrative check - residential staff saw this as least important, social workers ranked it as fifth out of the ten possible functions.

As 'monitoring' was the function which received the largest number of positive responses, perhaps we should expand on what the term 'monitoring' means. Monitoring can be used in at least two ways, both imply that it is a check on events - in this case on recent past events. The first usage of the term sees monitoring as a straightforward check: 'have we done

95

what we said we would do?', or 'have we followed the regulations?'. In its weakest form monitoring may thus be little
more than a recap of what has happened and in a sense may be
more appropriately allocated to the informational category.
In a second usage monitoring can be seen as evaluation; as
rigorously assessing the impact of previous decisions and
changing course if necessary. From what has already been said
about the content of reviews, and of area reviews in particular it was apparent in this study that the monitoring of
decisions, or casework, that takes place in reviews is <u>rarely
in the evaluative mode</u>.

When asked to choose the single most important function of
reviews in area offices and in residential homes, social
workers produced a reasonable consensus of opinion concerning
reviews in the latter - residential homes. Information
exchange was seen as the single most important function by a
majority of respondents. Long-term planning was the only other
function to be mentioned a significant number of times.
Replies to this question in relation to reviews in area
offices produced a more diffuse pattern of responses.
'Informing the Area Director of input' was the function which
was seen as most important by most social workers, but long-
term planning and decision-taking followed very closely behind.

Several respondents explained their choice of the single
most important function as being that function which was least
well covered by other social work activities. For instance,
many of the functions of reviews can equally be applied to
supervision sessions; if reviews are to serve purposes over
and above those of supervision then one would expect that
those functions which social workers do not see as appropriate to supervision should be given prominance in the review
situation. This observation highlights the relationship
between reviews and other aspects of social work practice, and
therefore the need for clarity in establishing the purpose of
these different aspects.

SOCIAL WORKERS' SATISFACTION WITH REVIEWS

Having recorded the functions they thought that reviews ought
to fulfil, social workers were then asked to indicate their
level of satisfaction with reviews in fulfilling those functions. Social workers' satisfaction is of course related to
their present understanding of the purposes of reviews. This
understanding may be based on a very general acceptance of
'that's how things are done here', rather than on any purposeful or deep thinking. Indeed, while working within the
area offices several social workers commented that until

questioned in connection with this research they had never previously considered or thought about reviews in this way. The social workers in this sample showed a clear satisfaction with the way reviews fulfilled the functions of monitoring, checking on the administration, and information exchange. However, they showed much less satisfaction with reviews in carrying out those functions which relate to planning, i.e. in making long-term plans, the systematic reassessment of earlier plans and in making decisions more specific.

These results may reflect the increasingly defensive stance taken by many Social Services Departments, generated by concern over media exposure, such as that reported in Chapter 1. This, together with criticisms such as those in the recent DHSS (1982) study of the Boarding Out of Children, tend to concentrate on the more measurable aspects of social work, such as fulfilment of regulations, rather than the more intangible qualities of casework or planning.

The discussion thus far has been based on the responses from social workers to questions on reviews in general. We now turn to the information relating to individual reviews. Detailed analysis of these results gives several bases of comparison: between what the researcher thought the review was about and what the participants thought; between what social workers thought actually happened and should have happened; between residential reviews and area reviews; between social workers in different area offices; and between individual social workers. A summary of some of the findings follows below.

RESEARCHERS' ASSESSMENT OF REVIEW FUNCTIONS

One might well expect that all reviews would have some minimum functions which almost by definition would occur every time, e.g. one could say that all reviews must at least involve some form of information exchange. Our use of the word function, however, does assume some, even if small, measure of considered purpose. Viewed thus, there was no single function that appeared to occur on every occasion, though at reviews held in area offices (when only the social worker and reviewer were normally present) the researcher identified two functions in the great majority of cases, namely 'administrative' and 'informational'. At the area office reviews the case records are presented and review forms scrutinised before signing. The check on case records may not always have been thorough, but mostly was sufficiently purposeful to be recorded as a function of the review. No other functions came close to these in their frequency; the next two functions which could be said to have occurred to some extent, if not as the dominant purpose, in at least half of the reviews were those of 'monitoring' and 'supervisory'. The functions relating to decision-making were much less in evidence - if ranked by frequency they appear as:

6th making new decisions
7th long-term planning
8th more specific decisions
9th reassessment of previous decisions

The ranking of the functions of reviews is strongly supported by the data which has already been presented in Table 8.3, which sets out the best overall description of both the review discussions and the decisions.

Since well over 3/4 of the reviews were described as maintenance of the status quo, short-term, or holding, it is not surprising that functions relating to decision-making were less prominent than those relating to information or monitoring. This is not to suggest that one would hope or expect to find all reviews producing new decisions or long-term plans. However, if long-term plans have been developed already then a review session would seem to be an appropriate occasion systematically to reassess or evaluate these plans. In fact, this function was even less evident, further supporting the contention that the monitoring which was taking place was of a limited nature.

WHAT SOCIAL WORKERS THOUGHT HAPPENED IN REVIEWS

There was no one function that all social workers thought applied to all reviews. The function which social workers saw as happening most often was that of monitoring and this was seen as occurring only 50% of the time. Closely following this came 'administrative checks' and 'informational'. The higher incidence of information rather than monitoring that was observed by the researcher, in comparison to that reported by social workers, can be explained by the researcher's previously expressed opinion that if the monitoring is of a very low order it is little more than information exchange. There are only two other notable differences in the recording of the researcher and the social workers. The latter saw long-term planning as occurring slightly more frequently, and the supervisory function occurring much less frequently than did the researcher. The hypothesis we would suggest to explain the former is that social workers are very aware of the highly volatile world of many of their clients and there-

fore tend to regard a year or two ahead as long-term, from a
planning point of view, whereas those viewing children in care
from the outside tend to see the long-term as stretching
towards adulthood.

The different perceptions of the importance of the supervisory function may be semantic and conceptual in that supervision has a specific meaning to social workers and may
relate in particular to the checking and development of
detailed casework plans - which is something none of the
reviewing officers in this sample saw as an appropriate
activity for a review session. However, if the supervisory
function refers to a general check of the social worker input
into a case, then this was apparent in many reviews. Indeed,
content analysis of the reviewing officers' questioning shows
a dominance of 'probing of social worker's input'. Furthermore, Area Directors expressed the opinion in interviews that
they used reviews, especially those organised in batches by
caseload, to make an overall assessment of the social worker's
work. As one Area Director said:

> they provide an opportunity to assess the performance of
> the social worker and the nature and quality of the
> supervision being provided by the senior.

Does this level of supervision appear contrary to the
development within social work of those characteristics
associated with professionalisation, in particular individual
autonomy based on the exercise of professional judgement?
Social workers operate from an organisation that more than
most is exposed to a high level of public accountability:
the exercise of individual professional judgement on the
development of casework plans and client interaction must
therefore be tempered with supervision by those held responsible. In this respect it is interesting to contrast the
reviews held in area offices with those held in residential
homes. In the latter situation both the researcher and the
social worker saw supervision as being a very unimportant,
almost a non-existent, aspect of the reviews. Here we have a
group discussion where several areas of expertise are
represented, there is no single hierarchical structure and the
workers are distanced from each other by training, organisation, fields of responsibility, etc. In such a situation the
ethics of 'professionals' do not allow for public criticism
of each other's work (although such criticism was often
expressed outside the review situation) and hence review
discussion is restrained by the need to maintain a consensus.

WHAT SOCIAL WORKERS THOUGHT SHOULD HAPPEN IN REVIEWS

By comparing social workers' responses to the question, 'what
was the main concern of this review' and 'what should have
been the main concern of this review', we have some measure
of social workers' satisfaction with reviews and ways in
which their expectations of a review differed from the
actuality.

The highest level of dissatisfaction in area office reviews
was with the administrative function, followed by 'decision-
making' and 'long-term planning'. In forty-six reviews an
administration check occurred when the social worker thought
it shouldn't and on thirty occasions they thought long-term
planning did not occur when they felt it should. However,
not all the differences that occurred between expectation and
actuality, were in the same direction: for instance, while
there were thirty reviews at which new decisions were not made
when social workers thought they should have been, there were
also nineteen occasions on which the making of new decisions
was seen as a function fulfilled by the review when the
social worker thought that it was not appropriate. This once
again points to the divergence of opinion among those most
closely involved in the review process.

Does this diversity arise from differences in expectation
among the social workers, or from the wide range of child
care cases which necessitates widely differing reviews? When
the results of the questions on individual reviews are broken
down, it can be seen that more often than not a particular
social worker will see the same functions as being relevant
to all his or her reviews, regardless of the differences in
the cases. This is particularly true for functions such as
'administrative' and 'supervisory' and least true for decision-
making functions - in particular whether a review is used to
make new decisions. These results are what one might expect,
as the former two functions can be seen to be related to
'style' while decisions are more case specific. Overall, the
divergences in responses to these questions are the product
of differences in the style and the expectations of individual
social workers, even from within the same area, rather than
differences in individual cases.

RESIDENTIAL REVIEWS

When we contrast residential reviews with those in area offices
there is much more consensus both within and between the
responses to all the different questions. It would seem that

social workers have a clearer idea of the purpose of residential reviews and are more likely to be satisfied with them. Furthermore, the functions of residential reviews as seen by the social worker, the researcher and the residential officer-in-charge are substantially different to those of area office reviews. The administration checking function and the supervisory function are of much less importance. There is the same difference of opinion between the researcher and the social worker about the relative importance of monitoring and information exchange; however, the most important difference recorded is in the emphasis given to long-term planning and to making new decisions. In fact the highest level of agreement from the social worker response to questions on what did happen and what should happen in reviews was on the function of making new decisions within residential reviews. The higher standing of functions related to decision-making and long-term planning within residential reviews raises some interesting questions.

We have already discussed in Chapter 7 the major differences between the organisation of residential reviews and those held in area offices. In contrast to area office reviews, a residential review is established much more formally as a decision-making occasion; the costs involved are higher; the opportunities of repeating or having an alternative occasion are much less, which increases the need for positive decision-making; the reviewing officer is more able to take the role of independent chairman; to the social worker (though not necessarily to the residential staff or reviewing officer) it is a one-off review, rather than one of a batch. Thus residential reviews have more of a 'case-conference type' structure and are more likely to be decision-making occasions.

A further reason why residential reviews are more often a forum for making decisions is the nature of a residential placement, in particular in an observation and assessment centre. Increasingly, residential care is seen as only a phase in the career of a child in care, particularly for younger children. Therefore the emphasis of many residential reviews must be to look for alternative and longer-term placements. All the work that has followed from the original 'Children Who Wait' study (Rowe & Lambert, 1973) has engendered a sense of the need for positive thinking for children in residential care. The evidence from many, but by no means all, of the residential reviews included in this study confirms this more positive attitude.

One possible conclusion to be drawn from this is the need for area reviews to adopt a similar case conference type structure if they are to engender the same positive attitude

to decision-making and planning. This would greatly
increase the costs incurred in conducting reviews, which would
have to be balanced against the increased possibility of
achieving the purposes which reviews set out to fulfil.
However before such an assessment could be made the purposes
of reviews would have to be clarified and made explicit. One
must also bear in mind that the enhancing of the role of
decision-making does not in itself mean that the decisions
taken will be more successfully implemented, as we shall see
later.

CONCLUSIONS

The first conclusion to be drawn is that reviews are multi-
functional; they have no single overriding purpose, but fulfil
several functions. Does this suggest that the various
purposes for reviews that have been expressed in the literature
may in fact be complementary? The evidence from this study
does not entirely support this view, largely because of the
lack of consensus among members of social work area teams.
They expressed very diverse opinions on the functions most
appropriately performed by reviews. Many would agree that
reviews have a monitoring function, as illustrated by the
social worker who said:

> The Social Services Departments see reviews as a means of
> making sure statutory requirements are met, as a means of
> tightening up the system and detecting potential flash
> points.

However the disagreement over the purpose of reviews can be
seen from the following quotations expressing the opinions of
two social workers from the same area office:

> In most child care cases long-term plans can be recognised,
> but it shouldn't be for the review to do this.

> I see the review as an instrument for recording major
> changes to long-term plans - no individual should be in
> the position of making long-term plans without the resort
> to other members of the team.

Are these differences derived from the diverse nature of the
cases subject to review or from the opinions of individual
social workers? The detailed analysis of responses to each
case suggests that the relevance of certain functions does
differ slightly between cases, but is more likely to differ
between the perceptions of individual social workers even
within the same area office. Several respondants explained
this uncertainty about the purpose of reviews by the lack of
clear direction from management. Although there was an under-

standing that management saw it as important to conduct reviews within the regulations, there was not the same clear
appreciation of what was expected from reviews or how they
related to other aspects of the social work task.

Turning now to the analysis of the functions of reviews, the
administrative, information exchange, and monitoring functions
were more in evidence in area office reviews than were
functions associated with decision-making or planning. Only
in a minority of cases were area office reviews used to make
new decisions and even less often to formulate long-term
plans. This suggests that reviews may be more accurately
viewed as decision-taking rather than decision-making
occasions.

Another important conclusion to be drawn from these responses
and observations is the marked difference between residential
reviews and area office reviews in what actually happens, in
what social workers think should happen, and in their level
of satisfaction with what happens. In brief, there is much
greater emphasis in residential reviews on decision-making
and much less on administrative or supervisory activity.
There is nothing in the statutory requirements for conducting
reviews that suggests that those which take place in residential homes should be any different in purpose from those conducted in area offices. The marked differences in function
shown in this research highlights again the lack of clear
guidelines from policy makers on the functions of statutory
reviews.

10 The nature of the decisions

INTRODUCTION

In the last three chapters we have concentrated on reviews as
the forum for decision-making. We now turn to the decisions
themselves. As shown in Chapter 3, the literature on decision-
making points to the importance of the nature of the decisions.
For instance, several writers suggest that the style of
decision-making which it is most appropriate to employ will
vary with the nature of the decision to be taken. Hence, one
aim that this research set out to fulfil was the development
of a typology of review decisions. Furthermore, so little is
known about review decisions that the application of such a
typology is important for two reasons: first, it provides a
fuller understanding of the decisions taken in reviews and
hence enables us to place review decisions within the total
decision-making process; second, it enables us to ascertain if
the nature of the decision is an important factor in the
successful implementation of the decision.

In considering the description of the decisions taken at
reviews it is important to bear in mind the situation in which
these decisions are being taken. Reviews take place at set
intervals, independent of the child's situation; they are not
called in response to a need to make new decisions and in that
sense could be seen as an artificial decision-making process.
However, although decision-making in child care is a continuous process, social workers will often postpone making a
decision until a review, if this is due to occur in the near
future. This may happen because they feel that decisions are
more appropriately taken by the Area Director or in a group,
as in residential reviews, rather than by an individual social
worker.

It is also worth restating at this point that we are looking
solely at the decisions as recorded on the review form. We are
not using the rest of the information on the form, or the
review discussion in support of or supplement to the decisions.
We should also restate here that this coding of decisions was
carried out by the researcher. While this classification was

as objective as possible, it must be accepted that there will be a subjective element.

In total, 894 decisions are included in this analysis:

284 were taken at reviews of cases held in Area X
397 were taken at reviews of cases held in Area Y
213 were taken at reviews of cases held in Area Z

However, as we have already demonstrated, reviews that take place in residential homes are of a very different character from those held in area offices, so a breakdown of the decisions on these lines will be of interest. Of the total of 894 decisions recorded,

175 or 19.6% were taken at residential reviews
719 or 80.4% were taken at area office reviews

These 894 decisions were taken at 298 reviews, giving an average of three decisions taken at each review, within a range of one to eight decisions. If a review produces several decisions it is likely that some will be more important than others - it is certainly unlikely that all the decisions will be highly important. Nonetheless, in this analysis all decisions are treated independently.

THE DECISIONS TYPOLOGY

The review decisions are described in seven major ways. These are:

1. The level of impact of the decision
   - on the child's life style or situation
   - on the child/social worker relationship
2. The type of decision - new, modified or repeat
3. The specificity of the goals
4. The specificity of the action
5. The expected time-scale for implementation, if this has been included
6. The primary focus of the content of the decision
7. The social work activity likely to follow from the decision

Each decision was categorised by the researcher on these seven dimensions. The results of this categorisation are reported below.

1. The impact of the decision

As mentioned previously, this analysis treats each decision as independent, rather than taking a review as a whole, therefore we can expect to find that the decisions vary in their level of significance. However, it is important to differentiate the decisions in some way. The measure that has been chosen in this research is the level of impact of the decision on the child's life style or situation, and on the child/social worker relationship. This measure minimises the significance of those decisions which reflect the status quo, and also decisions which relate to organisational aspects of the case-work and which don't impinge directly on the child.

As was noted in Chapter 3 differentiating decisions in this way was derived in part from Simon's distinction between programmed and non-programmed decisions (Simon, 1965). It will be interesting to see from the analysis that follows if decisions which we categorise as having a high impact on the child are of a different character from decisions with little impact on the child. But first let us see how the review decisions fit into this description.

The significance of the decisions was assessed in two ways, (a) the impact on the child in terms of his life style or future; (b) the impact on the social worker/child and family relationship. Only a small proportion of the decisions were assessed as having a major impact under either heading.

TABLE 10.1

The level of impact of the decision	Impact on the child	Impact on the social worker relationship
	%	%
Decisions which had a great impact	14.5	15.9
Decisions which had some impact	46.3	52.6
Decisions which had little or no impact	38.4	30.8

The range in the levels of impact of decisions on a child can be seen by comparing a decision such as 'continue the fostering introduction, with a view to R moving into the family for eventual adoption', which would be ranked as 'of great impact'. An example of a decision with little impact on the child is 'liaise with the health visitor'. Some decisions may have little impact on the child but may have a great impact in terms of social worker relations, e.g. 'initiate discussions about removing the child's name from the the 'at risk' register'.

The small number of decisions that are classified as 'having a great impact' is not in itself a reflection of the significance of the reviews. Indeed it would be an alarming situation if each review on a child called forth several major decisions. However, given a situation where the significance of the decisions varies, it is very necessary to classify them accordingly, so that the significance of the subsequent evaluation of the implementation of the decisions can be assessed meaningfully.

Impact on the child/place of review. We have already seen that reviews in residential homes are of a different character than those in area offices. Do these reviews also produce decisions that differ in the level of impact on the child?

TABLE 10.2

	Decisions which have a great impact on the child	Decisions which have some impact on the child	Decisions which have little impact on the child
Area office reviews	10.7	45.1	43.5
Residential reviews	30.3	51.4	17.1

We can see from Table 10.2 that there are very marked differences; these differences are statistically significant at a 1% confidence level. A much higher proportion of decisions made in residential reviews were seen as having a great or some impact on the child than was the case for decisions taken at area office reviews.

Throughout the rest of this chapter we shall return to these two variables - the level of impact of the decision and the place where the review was conducted. After discussing the decisions overall along each of the other dimensions, we shall examine the relationship between the nature of the decision and where it was taken and its impact on the child.

2. Type of decision

The second way in which the decisions were categorised was according to whether they were new, were repeated or were modified.

TABLE 10.3

Type of decision	Number	%
1. New decision because of a change in circumstances	132	14.8
2. New decisions: change in casework policy	339	37.9
3. Modified: made more specific	79	8.8
4. Modified: because of changes in circumstances	24	2.7
5. Repeated: still appropriate	233	26.1
6. Repeated: still to be implemented	32	3.6
7. Confirmation of a previous implicit decision	55	6.2
Total	894	100%

This can be summarised to show that:

    52.7% of all review decisions were classified as new
    11.5% of all review decisions were classified as modified
    35.9% of all review decisions were classified as repeated.

As over half of the review decisions were new, this would suggest that the review process must be seen as having a significant decision-making function.

However, when we refer to decisions as 'new' it does not necessarily imply that they arose solely out of the review discussion. It does mean that they were not previously recorded as part of the casework plan for that child - often particular courses of action will have been decided before a review, indeed may even be in operation, but the review is the formalisation of the decision-making. In this sense it may be truer to say that the review is often a decision-recording occasion rather than a decision-making one.

Decision Type/Review Type. Does the pattern of decision types vary according to where the review was held? Table 10.4 shows the percentage distribution of decision types for decisions taken at residential reviews and at area office reviews.

Table 10.4 shows that reviews on children in residential care produce more 'new' decisions and fewer 'repeat' decisions than those held in area offices. This confirms the findings of the

TABLE 10.4

Type of Decision	Area Office Reviews	Residential Reviews
1. New decision because of a change in circumstances	14.6	15.4
2. New decisions : change in casework policy	35.0	49.7
3. Modified: made more specific	9.0	8.0
4. Modified: because of changes in circumstances	2.5	3.4
5. Repeated: still appropriate	28.5	16.0
6. Repeated: still to be implemented	3.5	4.0
7. Confirmation of a previous implicit decision	6.8	3.4
	100%	100%

last chapter on the functions of reviews, which pointed to a much greater emphasis on decision-making in residential reviews. It also reinforces the description of almost half the area office reviews as 'maintaining the status quo,' and therefore more likely to have concentrated on monitoring past work than reassessing or planning future work.

Decision Type/Impact on Child. It is also of interest to know if the decision type is related to the impact of the decision on the child. This is shown in Table 10.5

If each decision type is broken down by their level of impact on the child, we find statistically significant differences. As one might expect, a higher proportion of decisions which had a large impact on the child were new decisions, and a lower proportion were repeat decisions. Table 10.5 also shows that a higher proportion of decisions with a large impact were repeated because they had not been implemented (7.7% compared to 3.6% for all decisions, 2.3% for decisions of little or no impact). It should be remembered here that 'decision type 6' refers to decisions which were originally taken at reviews previous to the one used for this research, but were repeated on this occasion through lack of implementation. Analysis of the rate of implementation of decisions recorded at the 'research review' also shows that decisions with a large impact on the child were less likely to be implemented or successfully implemented. Reasons why this might be so will be discussed later.

TABLE 10.5

IMPACT ON CHILD

DECISION TYPE	Large Impact	Some Impact	Little or No Impact	ALL DECISIONS
1. New decision because of a change in circumstances	10.0	13.3	18.1	14.8
2. New decisions: change in casework policy	60.0	38.6	29.4	37.9
3. Modified: made more specific	5.4	10.4	8.5	8.8
4. Modified: because of changes in circumstances	1.5	3.1	2.6	2.7
5. Repeated: still appropriate	11.5	27.1	29.7	26.1
6. Repeated: still to be implemented	7.7	3.1	2.3	3.6
7. Confirmation of a previous implicit decision	3.8	4.3	9.3	6.2

3. Specificity of goals

A great deal of the criticism that has surrounded social work has centred on the apparent lack of clear or meaningful objectives for working with clients (Goldberg & Warburton, 1979; Brewer & Lait, 1980). A review is one possible occasion in which such objectives can be made more specific. The aim of this classification is to see how far each decision contained a clear statement of goals. Decisions were classified into five categories as shown in Table 10.6.

The appropriate category in which to place a decision was not always obvious at a glance. Goals may have different timespans and different levels. Some decisions may detail what is to happen to the child at that point in time, but may not

TABLE 10.6

SPECIFICITY OF GOALS	% RESPONSES ALL DECISIONS
1. No goals apparent	10.2
2. Very general	15.9
3. General	29.9
4. Fairly specific	33.0
5. Very specific	11.1

offer any long-term objectives, e.g. 'child to remain in this home at present'. This could be said to have specified short-term goals; but no longer-term goals or does the decision only relate to action and not to goals at all? We have assumed goals to have a time-span beyond the present and therefore decisions like this have been classified as specific in terms of action, but general in terms of goals. The difficulties that are encountered in classifying these decisions by specificity of goals and of action would seem to arise from the confusion that exists in social work between ends and means. For instance two decisions which were frequently recorded were 'visit regularly' and 'support family'. Is 'to visit' or 'to support' an end, or a means to an end? Have social workers considered whether they are means or ends? Although one can understand that much of social work recording will be in a form of shorthand and carry implicit implications, the impression gained was that this form of shorthand may be a substitute for precision in defining aims and methods. As we can see from Table 10.6, allowing for the problems of classi-fication, the decisions are spread throughout the spectrum of specificity, with approximately 10% of the decisions containing no explicit goal and approximately 11% with clearly specified goals. 'Reconvene a case conference' is an example of a decision with no explicit goal, which can be compared with a decision with clear objectives 'to aim for a return to home by half-term'.

Specificity of goals and impact on the child. If this data on goal specificity is cross-tabulated with data on the 'impact on the child' we find that decisions which have a large impact on the child are much more likely to have greater specificity than those decisions of limited impact. For instance, if we look at the categories at each end of the continuum we find that of those decisions which have little impact, 27.4% are very general and 5.5% are very specific, whereas of those decisions which have a large impact only 9.2% are very general while 23.8% are very specific.

Specificity of goals and place of review. Table 10.7 shows the data on the specificity of goals of residential review and area office review decisions.

TABLE 10.7

	VERY GENERAL %	GENERAL %	SPECIFIC %	VERY SPECIFIC %	NO GOALS SPECIFIED %
Residential review decisions	9.7	30.9	32.0	10.3	17.1
Area office decisions	17.4	29.6	32.2	11.3	8.5

Perhaps the most notable feature of this table is the number of decisions taken at residential reviews that were classified as not specifying any goals. As explained earlier these are likely to be decisions that refer to immediate or short-term action, such as 'remain here at present'. However, if 'no goals' and 'very general goals' are taken together then the differences in the specificity of goals between residential decisions and area office decisions is slight.

4. Specificity of action

All decisions were placed into one of five categories, depending on the specificity of action. The result of this categorisation is shown in Table 10.8. This shows that decisions were classified throughout the spectrum, so that a very similar proportion of decisions were classified as general or very general, as were classified, as specific or very specific.

TABLE 10.8

SPECIFICITY OF ACTION	% OF ALL DECISIONS
1. No action apparent	2.1
2. Very general	19.7
3. General	29.1
4. Fairly specific	27.7
5. Very specific	21.4

Consideration of the specificity of action of review decisions raises questions about the relationship of reviews to
casework plans - there seemed to be general agreement in all
the social work areas researched that detailed casework plans
were not the concern of the review, but should be left to the
professional discretion of the social worker and senior.
Therefore a decision such as 'visit the foster home' will be
classified as non-specific in terms of the action, although it
is unlikely that the reviewer would see it as appropriate to
specify the number, timing, or purpose of home visits,
(although this did occur when senior social workers were the
reviewing officers). Another example of a decision which was
frequently recorded is 'support the foster parents': this is
another decision which is very non-specific in terms of action.
Can we assume that the social worker and reviewing officers
understand implicitly what is meant by this, or should we
expect a review to be more specific? The DHSS in 'Foster Care:
A Guide to Practice' points to the dangers of recording
decisions in an imprecise way:

> To ensure that the plan formulated at the review is
> executed, additional decisions will need to be made con-
> cerning the action required, the methods to be adopted and
> the individuals responsible for action. Unless reviews
> decide 'what, how and who', plans tend to remain written
> hopes on case records. (DHSS, 1976)

One might say that it is less necessary to spell out actions
in a review, if the goals are always clearly defined; as our
last piece of analysis showed this was far from being the case.
Detailed case plans may well be discussed by a social worker
and a senior in supervision sessions, but how often are these
recorded in the case file or social worker's notes? Observation suggests that this is not common practice. Observation
of the reviews would also suggest that a further reason for
the apparent reluctance to make decisions detailed specific
actions, is that social workers tend to see their cases as
fluid, even volatile, so casework plans must be equally fluid.
Again one can see the reasoning behind such an attitude - but
one can also see the ease with which fluid plans can become
non-existent and social worker activity becomes purely
reactive. Indeed one researcher quotes the reaction of the
local BASW group as follows:

> The BASW audience put forward the view that the conse-
> quences of child care decisions were so vital, and the
> alternatives so finely balanced, and the outcome so
> dependent on uncontrollable factors that social workers
> would not record or put forward their judgements and
> prescriptions for analysis, lest they prove faulty.
> (Robinson, 1981)

113

Another difficulty that arises with decisions that are non-specific in terms of their action, as well as their goals, is that of evaluating their implementation. For example, if a decision 'liaise with the health visitor' is recorded, one 'phone call to the health visitor in a six-month period could count as implementation of that decision. It could be said that the social worker knows how much liaison is appropriate to the situation, or that this can be decided by social worker and senior in supervision and it is not necessary to spell it out in a review. However, the same recording of a 'liaise with health visitor' decision can mean, in one instance, merely 'be aware that the health visitor is involved' but in another it can mean 'keep in very close touch as health visitor has vital information'. This underlines the limitations of the recording for research purposes and perhaps equally for professional purposes. As one of the major functions of these reviews is seen to be that of monitoring the casework since the last review, a firm statement of what is being monitored is important, if not essential. If decisions are recorded in a very non-specific style this task is harder to accomplish effectively.

Specificity of action/impact on child. As with specificity of goals, we find different distributions of specificity of action when crosstabulated with the level of impact on the child. Looking at the very general and the very specific categories we find that of decisions that have little impact on the child, 29.4% are very general and 15.5% are very specific. Whereas of decisions that have a major impact 12.3% are very general and 40.8% are very specific, showing that decisions with greater impact tend to be more specific than decisions with little impact.

Specificity of action and place of review. Crosstabulations of the specificity of action for residential review decisions and area decisions are shown in Table 10.9.

TABLE 10.9

PLACE OF REVIEW	VERY GENERAL %	GENERAL %	SPECIFIC %	VERY SPECIFIC %	NO ACTION SPECIFIED %
Residential review decisions	12.0	23.4	24.0	37.7	2.9
Area office review decisions	21.6	30.5	28.7	17.4	1.9

114

These results are in line with other findings which point to residential reviews as being different from area reviews – that difference being in their emphasis on decision-making, and in specific rather than generalised decision-making.

Specificity of action/specificity of goals. Before we leave this section on action we should consider the relationship between the specificity of goals and of action. Such an analysis shows that decisions which have very specific goals also tend to include specific actions and those with very general goals tend to include very general actions. However, a higher than expected proportion of those decisions which have no goals include very specific action. This tends to suggest that reviews may in part be leading to decisions which detail action as a substitute for goals.

5. Time-scale

If the implementation of a decision is to be effectively monitored, some indication is necessary of the expected time-scale for implementation. Good decision-making practice would also suggest the need to record how long one is prepared to allow for the successful implementation of one's plans before switching to an alternative. The essential importance of considering the time-scale of decisions has been well explained by BASW.

> Those who make decisions concerning future plans for children in care and more particularly those who have responsibility for implementing them, must always have regard to time-scale. Six months in the life of a baby or pre-school child cannot be compared with six months for an adolescent. Decisions which are made by default; whilst awaiting more information or other developments, are just as much "decisions" in their impact upon the child as properly planned and implemented programmes, only they are liable to lead to less satisfactory outcomes. Those responsible for reviews must never forget this basic tenet. (BASW, 1983)

When constructing this classification it was originally assumed that decisions would be categorised according to the length of time thought necessary to implement the decision. However, it soon became apparent that the primary classification would have to be based on whether or not there was any inclusion of a time-scale in the decision. Hence our classification of review decisions shows (a) Table 10.10: those decisions that mentioned a time scale and those that did not; (b) Tables 10.11 and 10.12: more detailed subdivision within those two categories.

115

TABLE 10.10
Inclusion of a time-scale

	% total cases
Time scale mentioned	21.7
Time scale not mentioned	78.2

TABLE 10.11
Decisions where time-scale is mentioned

	% OF DECISIONS WHERE TIME-SCALE WAS MENTIONED	% OF ALL DECISIONS
1. New decision, to be implemented immediately	15.0	3.2
2. New decision to be implemented within six months	58.0	12.6
3. New decision, to be implemented after six months	8.8	1.9
4. Ongoing decision - appropriate for the short-term	6.2	1.4
5. Ongoing decision - appropriate for the intermediate term	9.3	2.0
6. Ongoing decision - appropriate for the long term	2.6	0.6
Total	100.0	21.7

TABLE 10.12
Decisions where time-scale is not mentioned

	% OF DECISIONS WITH NO TIME-SCALE MENTIONED	% OF ALL DECISIONS
1. No planning	1.4	1.1
2. Impossibility of prediction	3.0	2.4
3. A new decision assumed to be acted on immediately	44.1	34.5
4. An ongoing decision assumed to be implemented while appropriate	51.4	40.2
Total	100.0	78.2

These results show that well over three quarters of the decisions did not include any time-scale for their implementation. Taken with the results of the two previous sections, this again points to the imprecise nature of the recording of review decisions.

It is perhaps not surprising to find that repeated decisions which are still ongoing have no time-scale included. What is more surprising is the number of new decisions that were recorded without any reference to timing. Most of these decisions carry the implicit assumption that they will be implemented immediately. When questioned on implementation of these decisions at least six months later, social workers were able to say that the majority had been implemented. However, this was often after five or six months, rather than immediately after the review. If the time-scale is not made explicit when recording the decision, then it is impossible effectively to monitor or evaluate the implementation of the decision.

As with the previous classifications of decisions, we can cross-tabulate the decisions by time-scale and the impact of the decision on the child and also present the findings for area and residential reviews.

Time-scale and impact on the child.

TABLE 10.13

	% DECISIONS WITH GREAT IMPACT	% DECISIONS WITH SOME IMPACT	% DECISIONS WITH LITTLE IMPACT	% ALL DECISIONS
Time-scale mentioned	38.5	21.6	15.4	21.8
Time-scale not mentioned	61.5	78.3	84.7	78.2

From this we can see that decisions with a great impact are more likely to have some measure of the time-scale for implementation included within the decision.

Time-scale and place of review. The results shown in Table 10.14 are again in line with those in the two previous sections, that decisions taken at residential reviews tend to be more precise or at least to be recorded more precisely.

TABLE 10.14

	% OF AREA DECISIONS	% OF RESIDEN- TIAL DECISIONS	% OF ALL DECISIONS
Time-scale mentioned	18.9	33.5	21.8
Time-scale not mentioned	81.1	66.5	78.2

6. Focus of decision

In this section and the next, attention is concentrated on the nature of the social work task. The next section will consider the specific social work activity that arises from the decisions. This section is more concerned with the nature of the social work intervention - on the aspect of the client's life the social worker hopes to have an influence. Inevitably many decisions taken at reviews do not directly concern social work with the client, but relate to administrative or organisational tasks that arise from the social worker's responsibility as an agent of a social services department, e.g. 'to retain a case on the 'at risk' register, or from their need to co-operate or to liaise with other agencies, e.g. 'talk to B's teacher'. In this study 35.8% of all decisions were placed in this category by the researcher (Table 10.15).

It would be reasonable to assume that social workers have more success in effectively implementing decisions that are orientated to the organisation or directed at influencing the child's environment. These are areas where one expects the social worker to have more control over actions and hence outcomes. Intervention that aims to influence the individual's personality or relationships is less in the control of the social worker and hard work in this sphere may bring little success.

Analysis of the level of success in implementation of the decisions only partially bears out these assumptions (explanation of the research method in assessing successful implementation is explained fully in Chapter 11); Table 10.16.

There is a slightly lower rate of success in implementing decisions directed at the client's personality or relationships and a higher level for decisions which are organisation orientated. However, there is also a lower level of implementation of decision related to the child's environment (27.3% 'not at all successful', compared with 20.7% overall).

118

Most of these decisions will be related to the deployment of resources to improve the child's environment - e.g. a move to a more suitable placement or the use of nursery or 'Homestart' facilities. These were rarely decisions that were ineffective because of the non co-operation of the client; the problem was that members of the review were making decisions on the basis of assumptions about resources which proved to be inaccurate or beyond the control of the social worker. This question of resources will be raised again when we look more fully at the implementation of decisions in the next chapter.

TABLE 10.15

	% OF ALL DECISIONS
Client Orientated:	
Action directed to influence the individual's personality and/or attitudes	2.8
Action directed to influence the quality of relationships	15.0
Action directed to influence the client's environment	30.1
Action which is a combination of these	15.7
Action which is orientated to the organisation	35.8

TABLE 10.16

IMPLEMENTATION	ALL DECISIONS	CLIENT ORIENTATED			A COMBINATION OF THESE THREE	ORGANISATION ORIENTATED
		TO INFLUENCE PERSONALITY	TO INFLUENCE RELATIONSHIPS	TO INFLUENCE CHILD'S ENVIRONMENT		
Not at all successful	20.7	25.0	17.4	27.3	12.6	19.8
Partially successful	17.4	25.0	28.3	16.3	18.9	12.1
Fully successful	61.9	50.0	54.3	56.3	68.5	68.1

7. Social work activity

There have been many attempts in recent years to define more closely the elements of the social work task; the Barclay Committee being one such example. This is seen as important at several levels: in helping to formulate broad social policies; in managing the social service organisation and in controlling resources; in helping individual social workers to plan and organise their casework. The results of this study can add further to the descriptions of the activities of social workers.

Data was collected for each decision taken, showing all social work activity that was likely to arise from the implementation of that decision, and also the one most important activity.

The list of social work activities that was employed was taken directly from that developed by Goldberg and Warburton (1979). Working from the National Institute of Social Work, Goldberg and Warburton developed a computerised case review system that would provide information on 'what the social worker did'; on the clients, the nature of their problems; resources available to social workers; liaison with other agencies etc. They hoped that this information could then be used to plan and rationalise the work at the individual social worker level, the team level, and the area office level.

Goldberg and Warburton, however, also felt that their case review system, which not only asked about past activities but also future plans and aims for cases, was a valuable exercise in increasing the objectivity, the decision-making and planning capabilities of social workers. However, in comparing the data collected by Goldberg and Warburton, with that in the study reported here, we shall only use those data which relate to 'social work activities undertaken since the last review'.

Goldberg and Warburton divided their results into cases held by intake and long-term teams and by client group. Hence we can compare the recording of the activity of members of a long-term team on child care cases - 111 cases of children in long-term care and 200 cases of children and families with problems. These give a selection of cases that is very comparable to our own. Goldberg and Warburton asked social workers to record, for each case, their social work activity in the past six months, given a check list of 10 possible activities. This is obviously not identical to assessing the activity likely to arise from individual review decisions as recorded in this study.

TABLE 10.17

SOCIAL WORK ACTIVITY	% DISTRIBUTION OF ACTIVITIES REPORTED BY GOLDBERG AND WARBURTON ON 311 CASES	% DISTRIBUTION OF ACTIVITY ARISING FROM 894 REVIEW DECISIONS
1. None	–	7.1
2. Exploratory/ assessment	14.0	12.8
3. Information/advice	13.4	14.2
4. Mobilising resources	11.8	11.5
5. Advocacy	4.8	2.2
6. Education in social skills	–	1.2
7. Check up/review visiting	26.5	13.4
8. Facilitating problem solving	17.9	18.9
9. Sustaining/nurturing	11.8	17.0
10.Group activities	–	1.8

While the distribution of these two sets of figures is not exactly the same, they do follow a fairly similar pattern. Goldberg and Warburton report a greater amount of review visiting but less 'sustaining and nurturing' - these may often be part and parcel of the same activity, so perhaps the difference is not as great as the figures first suggest.

The wide range of activities arising from review decisions an and their comparability to the recording of all social worker activity with children and families reported by Goldberg and Warburton suggests that all aspects of child care practice are covered by reviews. One would certainly expect the review discussion to cover all aspects of a child care case, especially given the emphasis on monitoring that has been noted. What is possibly more surprising is that the review decisions - which are the basis of this activity analysis - should also cover such a broad area of activity.

CONCLUSIONS

The results presented here show that review decisions vary considerably in their character. One each of the seven dimensions assessed the whole range of categories was used, although the proportions in each category differed considerably. When this is added to the multifunctional aspect of reviews, it suggests that it may be misleading to perceive reviews as a single type of activity. Instead it may be necessary to categorise reviews into several types. This would then make it possible to vary the decision-making process according to the nature of the decisions to be made at that review.

Furthermore, against what is regarded as good decision-making practice, a high proportion of these decisions were recorded in a vague way. They contained low levels of specificity of goals, of actions and of timing. As already noted, such high levels of generality make effective monitoring of such decisions already difficult. Similarly, because of this lack of detail in the decisions, social workers may find reviews to be of little benefit when developing their case-work plans. Indeed, this may partly explain the observation that little use was made of reviews once they had been completed.

Once again a major conclusion from the set of results reported in this chapter is the differences between area office reviews and residential reviews.

A summary follows of the main differences between decisions taken in these different locations.

- A much greater proportion of residential decisions (30.3%) were assessed as having a great impact on the child, compared to 'area decisions',(10.7%).
- A much greater proportion of area decisions (43.5%) were assessed as having little impact on the child, compared to (17.1%) in residential decisions.
- A greater proportion of residential decisions (65.1%) were 'new'.
- A greater proportion of area decisions (32.0%) were 'repeat'.
- A greater proportion of residential decisions (37.7%) were very specific in terms of action.
- A greater proportion of area decisions (21.6%) were very general in terms of action.
- A time-scale for implementing the decision was included in 33.5% of residential decisions, and only in 18.9% of area decisions.

These results continue the pattern established in previous chapters of the very different character of residential reviews compared to area office reviews. These differences reinforce the picture of residential reviews as a more effective decision-making forum.

Taken together, these analyses of the nature of review decisions suggests that at reviews the reviewing officer is attempting to draw up a synoptic casework plan, including not only major changes, but also minor or continuing activities. This is a legitimate function for reviews to perform. However, as was noted earlier none of the reviewing officers saw reviews as the appropriate place to make detailed casework plans - the limited specificity of action in the decisions confirms this. What is happening is that review decisions cover the general areas in which the social worker will work but do not spell out detailed casework plans. More importantly they are also unlikely to spell out clearly the objectives that these social work activities aim to achieve.

11 Implementation of review decisions

One starting point for this research was the expressed concern with the apparent lack of implementation of review decisions. Assessment of the level of implementation of review decisions was therefore an important aim of this study, and it is the result of that assessment which is now reported. In the previous chapter the analysis of the nature of these decisions pointed to the imprecise way in which the majority of review decisions were recorded. From this one could argue that the decisions do not contain the criteria necessary for an evaluation of the implementation. It is important, therefore, to recognise what this study is evaluating and how this has been assessed. In assessing the implementation of the review decisions we are not evaluating either the quality or the success of the casework that the social worker had undertaken. What we are assessing is the extent to which the social workers saw themselves as implementing the decisions as recorded in the review. Furthermore, we asked the social workers to assess the implementation of the decisions in two ways:

- firstly, the extent to which they performed the actions appropriate to or specified in the review decision;
- secondly, the extent to which the aims or outcomes specified or implicit in the decisions were achieved.

It is important to make clear that the measurement of the extent of implementation of the decisions which is reported in this chapter is based on the social workers' own responses to a questionnaire on each decision. Although the social workers completed the questionnaires, they were administered personally by the researcher. The social workers were aware that the researcher had a good knowledge of each case from reading the case notes and from attending the reviews. The respondents were asked to assess the level of implementation of decisions which had been recorded in a review. From the discussion of the previous chapter it will be clear that we must be cautious in assuming that the decisions as recorded are a true reflection of the action intended or implicit when the decision was taken.

125

Social workers were asked to answer two main questions for each review decision:

    (i)   Did you work towards implementing this decision?
    (ii)   How far do you think the decision has been successfully implemented and achieved its aims?

The choice of responses to each question was the same - not at all; partially; fully. These questionnaires were completed by the social worker at least six months after the decisions had been taken, when the next review of the case had taken place. Table 11.1 gives the distribution of responses to question (i) - we shall subsequently refer to this as 'implementation'.

TABLE 11.1

	NUMBER OF DECISIONS	% OF ALL DECISIONS
Not implemented	81	9.3
Partially implemented	104	12.0
Fully implemented	683	78.7
Total	868	100%

Table 11.2 gives the distribution of responses to question (ii) - we shall subsequently refer to this as 'successful implementation'.

TABLE 11.2

	NUMBER OF DECISIONS	% OF ALL DECISIONS
Not successfully implemented	174	20.2
Partially successful	152	17.6
Fully successful	537	62.2
Total	863	100%

The figures from these two tables deserve some comment, even before they are broken down for more detailed analysis. The first point to note is that in less than 10% of cases has the social worker not worked in some measure towards implementation. Given that this could have occurred for several reasons (which are discussed below), this must count as a high level of decision implementation. Looking now at the second table we see that, as one would expect, the level of successful implementation is lower than the level of implementation.

One-fifth of decisions were not at all successful, although more than three-fifths were successfully implemented. Again this is a high level of successful implementation. However, this level of implementation must be seen in relation to the nature of the decisions involved and to the rigorousness of the evaluation criteria.

As we have seen, the decisions as recorded generally were very low in their level of specificity of goals, of action and of time-scale. This therefore leaves the criteria for evaluation of implementation exceedingly loose. For example, if a decision reads 'support foster family', but does not detail why, or how or when this is to be done, as little as one visit in a six-month period could qualify as 'working towards implementation'. If there were no major upheavals in the case, this could also qualify as having been 'successfully implemented and achieved its aims'. Furthermore, the majority of decisions recorded did not specify a date by which implementation could be expected. For many of these it was assumed that implementation should take place immediately. However, as the recording of the rate of implementation occurred at least six months after the decision was taken, many of these decisions which have been processed as being fully implemented disguise the degree of slippage in the intended time-scale for implementation.

REASONS FOR NON-IMPLEMENTATION

Let us now consider the reasons why the social workers failed to implement some of these decisions. Based on the pilot studies and observation of past reviews, six possible reasons for non-implementation were identified, which are listed in Table 11.3 below. Using this list, social workers were then asked 'If a decision was not fully implemented was it for any of the following reasons?' Their responses to this question, which relate to the 17.3% of the decisions not fully implemented, are given in Table 11.3.

TABLE 11.3

REASONS FOR NON-IMPLEMENTATION	NO.	%
1. Lack of time	39	20.9
2. Did not agree with the decision	14	7.5
3. A change of circumstances	42	22.4
4. A long-term decision; no action needed	16	8.6
5. An oversight	17	9.1
6. A change of casework plans	20	10.7
7. Other	39	20.9

Under the 'other' category were included decisions where the social worker did not act because the client, friends or other agencies carried out the necessary task for themselves, e.g. 'Ask the housing department about re-housing'. Also included under this category are decisions which suggested alternative courses of action which proved unnecessary - e.g. 'if x happens then do y'; however, if x did not happen, then y and the decision as a whole was redundant.

'A change of circumstances' refers to changes which were outside the social worker's control, e.g. if a young person reoffended or a parent failed to visit. Given that the actual time-scale for implementing many of these decisions was longer than that intended at the time the decision was taken, one could argue that there is an increased likelihood of circum- stances changing. This was exactly the point being made by BASW in the quote on page 115. In this sense 'changes of circumstances may not be entirely outside the social worker's control.

The categories which point directly to a lack of social worker input are lack of time; oversight; didn't agree with the decision - these categories applied to 70 decisions, or 8% of the total decisions. This suggests a very high level of effort to implement review decisions.

REASONS FOR LACK OF SUCCESS IN IMPLEMENTATION

Let us now look at the reasons for failure to implement successfully, based on responses to the second question. Under this heading we shall look at not only those decisions which the social worker did not implement, but also those which the social worker tried to implement but without success. Table 11.4 shows the distribution of the reasons for non-implementa- tion of those decisions. (There are 385 entries, as on occasion more than one reason was cited in relation to a single decision.)

This table points to two major reasons for lack of success in social worker intervention: (a) lack of co-operation, and (b) lack of resources.

Lack of co-operation

The term 'lack of co-operation' is being used to refer to both deliberate obstruction and also to situations where the child or the family or agency are unable to co-operate. The lack of success with these decisions demonstrates that often a social

TABLE 11.4

REASONS FOR NON-SUCCESSFUL IMPLEMENTATION OF DECISIONS	NO.	%
1. The decisions was a long-term one; the time-scale was too short for implementation	34	8.8
2. Lack of resources within Social Services Department	23	6.0
3. Lack of resources other than Social Services Department	15	3.9
4. Lack of social work input	43	11.2
5. Decision became inappropriate because of changes in circumstances	63	16.4
6. Decisions became inappropriate because of changes in casework plans	23	6.0
7. Lack of co-operation of child	54	14.0
8. Lack of co-operation of child's family	65	16.9
9. Lack of co-operation of other agencies	30	7.8
10. Other	35	9.0
Total	385	100.0

worker makes plans which involve intervention in a situation
where he cannot control the outcome. This may be in relation
to individual behaviour, (e.g. 'Encourage Mrs B. to visit her
daughter in her foster home') or to liaise with other agencies,
(e.g. 'ask the school to consider accepting this child'). In
instances such as these the social worker may expend considerable time and effort but in the end the success of this
effort depends on the activities of others.

Is this lack of co-operation related to lack of participation by the client in decision-making? In Chapter 2 we
reported the opinion of many workers in the child care field
that greater participation in reviews would increase their
effectiveness. A quotation from one of our social worker
respondents expresses this viewpoint clearly:

One reason for non-implementation of review decisions is
that the clients' viewpoint is not sufficiently taken into
consideration and consequently co-operation in implementing
a decision is not obtained.

Lack of resources

'Lack of resources' refers to resources both within the Social Services Department and to other resources. Those within the Social Services Department referred most often to placements or to places in an I.T. group; those outside referred most often to employment opportunities but also included housing and leisure activities. A 'lack of resources' was the reason for non-implementation in 10% of decisions. Just as the last paragraph demonstrated that a social worker's ability to implement decisions may be restricted by lack of control over others, so may it be restricted by his lack of control over resources. This situation arises when social workers make plans for children assuming or hoping that the resources will be there to meet those plans.

This, of course, does not take account of those occasions when a social worker may have preferred to make a different decision but was constrained from doing so knowing that the resources were most probably not available. Social workers were questioned about this for each case and also for each individual decision. When asked 'Are there any additional resources which, if available, would substantially alter your work on this case?' in 21.1% of cases an affirmative response was given. The question relating to individual decisions was: 'In some cases there may be constraints on making decisions based solely on professional judgement. In making this decision, how far do you feel professional judgement was constrained by other factors?' Of the responses to this question 12.4% pointed to some constraints, although only 5% of these were regarded as major. The respondents did not find these questions easy to answer. From discussions arising from this it seems that social workers' plans or even visions of how they could assist a client are very much tied to their experiences of existing resources. For example, those social workers who were dealing with very vulnerable 'at risk' children in an area with no day nursery facilities did not mention this as a constraint on their activities, although the existence of a day nursery would have had a major impact on their efforts in monitoring the case of vulnerable young children.

REVIEW ORGANISATION AND IMPLMENTATION RATES

One of the basic hypotheses of the research was that the subsequent implementation of decisions would be dependent on the structure of the decision-making unit. There were two major sources of variation in the structure of the review,

(1) the differences between residential reviews and area office reviews and (2) the differences between reviews held in each area.

(1) Residential/area review decisions

Table 11.5 shows the different rate of implementations of decisions, depending on where they were taken.

TABLE 11.5

	Not implemented	Partially implemented	Fully implemented
Decisions taken in Area Offices Reviews	8.1	11.6	80.4
Decisions taken in Residential Reviews	15.0	13.8	71.4

We can see that there is a difference in the rate of implementation between 'area' decisions and 'residential' decisions and this difference is statistically significant. There were proportionally more decisions taken in residential reviews which the social worker did not work towards implementing.

(2) Differences in reasons for non-implementation

Are there any differences in the reasons given for non-implementation? An examination of the responses shows that a smaller proportion of non-implemented decisions taken at residential reviews was due to 'lack of time' or 'oversight', but a larger proportion fell into the category 'other'. This most often related to decisions that the social worker thought the residential staff were responsible for implementing, e.g. 'To prepare D for independent living' or 'to restrict the contact that the child has with her home'. In residential reviews, where the structure is more akin to a case conference, it is of vital importance that responsibility for implementing a decisions is thoroughly discussed and understood. Difficulties can easily arise in decision-taking between field work staff and residential staff as there is no single, or clear, 'chain of command'. This situation is only overcome during the review, because both social worker and residential staff are present and are subject to the review chairman. If the opportunity to specify responsibility is missed at a review, the chances of the decision being effectively implemented will

131

be greatly lessened.

The difficulties of demaraction between field social workers and residential staff were appreciated by the Barclay Committee. While recognising the increasing professionalism and desire for greater autonomy for residential workers, Barclay warns of the dangers from lack of co-ordination.

> decisions may be better taken by the residential social worker who knows the child best ... but the crucial point here is that all concerned need to know who carries the authority and responsibility and why. These matters should not be left unclear or they will cause tension between the social workers to the detriment of the client. (Barclay, 1982)

Comparison of the different rates of successful implementation of decisions taken in area offices with those in residential homes, is given in Table 11.6.

TABLE 11.6

	Not at all successfully implemented	Partially successfully implemented	Fully successfully implemented
Decisions taken at area review	17.5	17.6	64.9
Decisions taken at residential review	32.5	17.5	50.0

Once again the differences are statistically significant, with a much smaller proportion of residential decisions being successfully implemented. Indeed only half of those decisions taken at residential reviews were fully implemented successfully.

The reasons given by the social workers for failure to implement the decisions were different for residential decisions than for decisions taken in area offices. The distribution of the responses for the two sets of decisions varies, in particular, at four points: 'Lack of social work input' and 'lack of co-operation of the child's family' appear much less often for residential decisions, but 'lack of resources', both inside and outside the Social Services Department appear much more often for residential decisions. When identifying the lack of resources within the Social Services Department, respondents referred most often to a shortage of suitable placements for children; the resources which they found lacking outside the

132

Social Services Department were mainly housing, employment or leisure activities for young people.

From observation of residential reviews it was clear that making decisions which depend on resources for successful implementation was problematic. The discussion often ranged around what would be best for the child at that immediate point in his career, and decisions were made accordingly - often with no clear idea if the necessary resources were available and rarely with any properly formulated alternative plan if the best option was not available, or not available at that point in time. It also seemed that this situation was made worse by the lack of knowledge by the participants, including even Care branch personnel, of the nature or extent of the resources that were available, even within the Social Services Department. Knowledge of particular institutions etc.did not seem to be gained in any systematic fashion, but rather through chance and rumour.

As was noted earlier all models of the decision-making process include the need to make choices between alternatives; such choices only being made after a search for possible alternatives. From observation of residential review dis- cussions it would seem that such a search was unnecessarily limited because of lack of information. The implications of this are well expressed by Parker et al.

> for a review group to be able to consider alternatives it has to possess good information about their availability and quality, as well as the capacity to think outside the standard range of provisions: especially to know about the changing circumstances of the child's family. This is not easy or inexpensive in terms of time or commitment. Nevertheless, that is the minimal price which has to be paid in order to forge a review system which really serves the best interests of the child rather than one which exists to place a routine seal of approval on the arrange- ments of the moment. (Parker, 1980)

Part of the apparent uncertainty of Wainshire social workers over the availability of places was due to the decision- making procedure and the lack of a 'single line of command'. With how much authority could a social worker or an Area Director request a place for one of their children? How far was the Head of Home able to say who they would or would not accept? However much the procedure may have had its own internal logic, undoubtedly the process of allocating resi- dential places meant that many important review decisions were taken with either a lack of information or authority to ensure they were successfully implemented.

In this context, aspects of the critique by Smith and Ames of the operation of social service teams seems relevant. These authors suggest that an examination of the extent of decentralised decision-making could be used to test the principle implicit in Seebohm that frontline units in social work require considerable autonomy. They conclude that:

> little purpose is served by offering teams of fieldworkers the formal authority to make decisions without also assigning to them the power of decision-making and ensuring that this power is exercised. (Smith and Ames, 1976)

Despite these reservations about limited search processes, where there is a genuine lack of resources, a choice between alternative placements may not be possible. This is not only a limitation to reviews but has consequences for all decision-making. Many of the respondents referred to the lack of resources and therefore to a lack of any real choice as a major inhibitor in the development of long-term plans for children in care.

COMPARISON OF THE THREE AREAS

Having compared the level of implementation of decisions taken in residential reviews with those taken in area offices, as a whole, let us now consider our second source of variation in the review structure, namely, different area offices. The level of implementation for decisions taken in each of the three social work areas is shown in Table 11.7

TABLE 11.7

	Decisions from AREA X	Decisions from AREA Y	Decisions from AREA Z	All decisions
Not implemented	7.8	9.5	11.6	9.3
Partially implemented	10.5	14.7	8.1	12.0
Fully implemented	81.6	75.8	80.3	78.7

Table 11.7 shows some variation in the rates of implementation of decisions with Area Y showing the lowest rates, but these differences are not statistically significant. There are, however, differences between the areas in the reasons for non-implementation. Area X has a greater proportion of decisions which were 'long-term; no immediate action required'. Area Y had a much greater proportion of decisions not implemented

through 'lack of time'; Area Z had very few of these but 'an oversight by social worker' did occur more often in this area, as did the response 'did not agree with the decision'; this was not once given as a reason in Area X. This is most likely due to the way in which review decisions were formulated; in Area Z the Area Director composed and recorded them at the review, in Area X the social worker came with them already drafted.

TABLE 11.8

	Decisions from AREA X	Decisions from AREA Y	Decisions from AREA Z	All decisions
Not at all successful	17.7	19.8	25.1	20.2
Partially successful	22.5	17.8	8.8	17.6
Fully successful	59.7	62.4	66.1	62.2

The results given in this table show statistically significant differences between the level of successful implementation of decisions taken in different areas. The results also show such variation as to make simple conclusions difficult. For example Area X has the lowest proportion of fully implemented decisions and also the lowest proportion of decisions not at all successfully implemented; Area Z has the highest proportion of fully implemented decisions and also the highest proportion of decisions not at all successfully implemented. There are two possible explanations of this result:

(i) the difficulties all the social workers experienced in distinguishing between the categories of not at all/ partially/fully successful when assessing the implementation of a decision.
(ii) the decisions taken in Area Z were somehow different from those in the other areas.

The second explanation seems to hold. Decisions taken in Area Z were more specific in terms of both goals and action. This may therefore make it easier for social workers in Area Z to assess whether their decisions were not at all or partially successful. This suggests that if greater specificity was used in formulating decisions then a greater number would be recognised as not at all successful.

To avoid the confusion over the distinction between 'not at all' and 'partially' implemented, these two categories can be merged, giving a basic classification of implemented/not imple-

mented. Similarly by merging the responses 'not at all successful implementation' and 'partially successful implementation' we have a basic classification of successfully implemen-
ted/not successfully implemented. When the results from the
three areas are examined in this way, we find that there are
no significant differences between the areas in terms of the
rates of successful implementation of review decisions.

FOSTER CARE AND REVIEW DECISIONS

Throughout this research the placement of children has been
categorised in four ways: fostered, in residential care, at
home-on-trial and at home. In a previous section we compared
the implementation of decisions taken in residential reviews
with those taken in area office reviews. This latter category includes children who are fostered, home on trial and
living at home. Those children in the latter category are not
bound, by statute, to be reviewed, hence much of the emphasis
in discussion of reviews in the child care literature has
concentrated on children who are fostered or are in residential care.

Therefore a comparison of the rates and success of implementation of decisions on these children may be of interest.
Table 11.9 shows the level of decisions implementation in
reply to question (i); Table 11.10 shows the level of successful implementation in reply to question (ii).

These tables show that review decisions on children in
foster care are much more likely to be implemented and successfully implemented than for children in residential care.

TABLE 11.9

	Not implemented	Partially implemented	Fully implemented
Children who are fostered	6.5	11.4	82.1
Children in residential care	15.0	13.8	71.3

The reasons given by social workers for ineffective implementation differ for these two groups of decisions, as shown
in Table 11.11.

TABLE 11.10

	Not at all successfully implemented	Partially successfully implemented	Fully successfully implemented
Children who are fostered	11.5	18.5	70.0
Children in residential care	32.5	17.5	50.0

TABLE 11.11

Reasons for unsuccessful implementation	Decisions on children who are fostered %	Decisions on children in residential care %
1. The decision was a long-term one; the time-scale was too short for implementation	16.9	9.2
2. Lack of resources within Social Services Department	2.5	10.2
3. Lack of resources other than Social Services Department	0.8	11.2
4. Lack of social work input	16.1	4.1
5. Decision became inappropriate because of changes in circumstances	19.5	16.3
6. Decisions became inappropriate because of changes in casework plans	5.9	2.0
7. Lack of co-operation of child	9.3	17.3
8. Lack of co-operation of child's family	11.9	8.2
9. Lack of co-operation of other agencies	10.2	7.2
10.Other	6.8	14.3

For children in foster care the decisions are more likely not to be implemented because they are long-term and insufficient time had elapsed to allow for implementation, and because of lack of social worker's effort. For children in residential care 'lack of resources' was more likely to be a cause of ineffective implementation, as we have already discussed in this chapter.

THE IMPACT OF THE DECISIONS AND LEVELS OF IMPLEMENTATION

In the previous chapter we examined the nature of review decisions along several dimensions. One of the ways in which the decisions were classified was according to the level of the impact of the decision on the child's life style or situation. We now want to consider whether the rate of implementation of the decisions varied according to the level of the impact of the decision. The figures relating to this are shown in Table 11.12.

TABLE 11.12

Implementation	IMPACT ON THE CHILD			All decisions
	Decisions with great impact	Decisions with some impact	Decisions with little impact	
Not at all	9.9	7.6	11.5	9.4
Partially	15.7	12.2	11.2	12.3
Fully	74.4	80.2	77.3	78.2

The figures relating to 'successful implementation' are shown in Table 11.13

TABLE 11.13

Implementation	IMPACT ON THE CHILD			All decisions
	Decisions with great impact	Decisions with some impact	Decisions with little impact	
Not at all	25.6	20.9	18.0	20.5
Partially	17.4	16.6	18.6	17.5
Fully	57.0	62.5	63.4	62.0

138

Neither of these tables show any statistically significant relationship between the level of impact of a decision and whether or not it was implemented, or successfully implemented. This may be a reflection of the review process and the measures used in assessing the rate of implementation of the decisions. Overall a very high proportion of decisions were assessed as 'fully implemented' and a small proportion as having a 'high impact on the child'. Perhaps these results also reflect the position where, with the exception of residential reviews, the same review process is used to make a large number of decisions which vary greatly in their character and which relate to a wide range of cases and circumstances.

CONCLUSIONS

The results presented in this chapter indicate when social workers made an assessment of the extent to which they saw themselves as implementing review decisions that a very high level of decision implementation, and a lower, but still high, level of successful implementation of decisions was recorded. In less than 10% of decisions did the social worker fail to work in some measure towards implementation. Overall, 62% of the decisions were successfully implemented, that is, achieved the aim implicit in the decision.

However, the complete picture is perhaps not as reassuring as these figures may at first suggest. There are two qualifications, in particular, which should be borne in mind. These are the imprecise nature of the review decisions and the much lower rate of successful implementation of decisions taken in residential reviews.

In the previous chapter the detailed description of the review decisions pointed to the significant lack of specificity in the decisions. This was true, in particular, for the goals, the action and the time-scale for implementation. There were many examples of general decisions, such as 'support the foster family', 'maintain some contact with B's siblings' or 'liaise with the school'. Because of the limited detailed requirements contained in these decisions the criteria for establishing effective implementation is similarily limited. For instance, is one visit in six months sufficient action for successful implementation of the decision to support the foster family? The answer to that question is not contained within the decision, neither is it possible to deny implementation.

Hence this generality of decision recording enhances the

levels of decision implementation which obviously limits the impact of this research analysis. But more importantly for social work practice, it also diminishes the opportunity for effective monitoring of reviews decisions within the area office.

However, the level of precision of decisions taken in residential reviews was much greater than that for decisions taken in area offices. Indeed it has been noted throughout this report that residential reviews differ from those conducted in area offices. Once again, in examining the extent of, and causes for, failure to implement decisions we find a significant difference. Decisions taken at residential reviews were less likely to be implemented and less likely to be successful than decisions taken in area offices. Indeed half the decisions taken in residential reviews were not successfully implemented.

From observation of residential reviews it would seem that three factors contributed to this greater failure to implement residential decisions, despite their greater emphasis on decision-making in residential reviews. First, in situations of uncertainty decisions were made which were based on insufficient information. Second, successful implementation required access to specific resources, which was an aspect over which the review had limited control. Third, residential decisions were often more ambitious and in reference to dynamic and therefore volatile circumstances. Ambitious decision-making in such a situation has a higher chance of failure, but if successful produces very substantial rewards. In discussing the responsibilities placed on social workers when dealing with child abuse cases, Hardiker and Barker suggest that the criteria for judging social worker decision-making should not be based solely on the assumption that they will always be right:

> working in conditions of uncertain outcome and high risk, a professional cannot be held accountable for providing correct solutions, but should be expected to use available knowledge in an ethical way. This implies a knowledge of theory and research performance skills and an attitude of service to client needs. This is no small undertaking, but it establishes manageable criteria for good decision-making, by contrast with the assumption that social workers should always be right. (Hardiker & Barker, 1981)

The implications of this for increasing the level of successful implementation of residential decisions would seem to be threefold:

1. The need for fuller preparation before a review on the

resource options which are currently available.

2. The need to decentralise decision-making on resources to allow the 'review' more control over resource allocation.

3. Good decision-making practice suggests that one way to avoid failure to implement is to ensure that decisions which are new, or which carry a high risk, include within them an alternative course of action should the first option become unobtainable.

12 The importance of reviews in child care practice

REVIEWS AND DECISIONS

The findings from the research that have been included in this
report, so far, relate specifically to the review process.
However, if implications are to be accurately drawn from an
evaluation of the reviews as a decision-making process, then
they must be placed within the context of the overall child
care decision-making and practice.

We saw in Chapter 3 that within the total casework on a
child the decision-making activity and the review process over-
lap, but by no means coincide. How far are reviews used as a
forum for making the important decisions on children in care?
Obviously the most important decision - that which initially
makes the child a 'reviewable case', - whether being taken
into care or being put under supervision - cannot be taken at
a review. Once a child becomes a reviewable case, how important are reviews in major decision-taking? A count was taken
of all the major decisions that had been taken in the past
year on all the cases included in the sample. (A major or
important decision was defined to include changes in legal
status, changes in placement, changes in parental contact.)
In just over half of these cases at least one major decision
had been taken, and in more than 1/7 two or more major
decisions had been taken. Of all these major decisions only
21% were taken at reviews; 28% were taken at case conferences
and 51% elsewhere (for example, in supervision or by the Court).
Although reviews played a part in the making of major decisions on children, therefore, this was not a dominant part.
This was equally true for children in residential care, despite
the greater emphasis on decision-making in residential reviews
that has been noticed earlier.

CASE CONFERENCES

Another element affecting the total decision-making context is
the case conference. Case conferences and reviews may appear,

at times, to be performing a similar task, especially when a
child or young person has recently been received into care.
However, specially convened individual case conferences are
not initiated for the same reasons as six monthly statutory
reviews. To treat these two meetings as a single type may
increase the confusion that exists among participants as to
their purposes. In this respect, one could dispute the
opinion expressed by the Children's Legal Centre when they say:

> We consider the terms 'reviews' and 'case conferences' to
> be synonymous, and mean any local authority-organised
> meeting at which decisions and plans about children in care
> are made. (Children's Legal Centre, 1983)

If case conferences are being used for different purposes, one
could assume that where they are a common part of child-care
practice reviews will be regarded as less significant. In this
study one child in six had been the subject of a case conference within the past year (although some of these may have been
held prior to the child becoming a 'reviewable case'). We have
commented earlier that many social workers would like to see
area reviews develop toward the style of a case conference, but
that this would cause major organisational changes. One
possible solution would be to combine the case conference and
review - or are the purpose of these meetings too dissimilar?
This would not, in general, improve the level of participation
in reviews by children and their families as case conferences,
as constituted at present, rarely include the child or his
family or foster family. Also in considering such a suggestion
one would have to be aware of the possibility of transferring
to the reviews, not only the advantages of the case conference
format, but also the disadvantages; in particular the problem
of meetings that are too large and too long (Hallet & Stevenson, 1980).

REVIEWS AND CASE WORK PLANS

We have seen that reviews only play a limited role in the
making of major decisions. What is the role of reviews in the
making of less fundamental decisions? It is impossible to
perform a similar exercise that would take into account all
child care decisions, so we asked social workers to assess the
importance of each review in translating broad aims into
implementable decisions. Table 12.1 shows their responses for
all reviews, for residential reviews and for reviews held in
each area.

The modal response was that reviews are 'fairly unimportant'
in making decisions - although the responses were spread
throughout the range. Comparisons between residential and area

TABLE 12.1

The importance of reviews in making decisions	All reviews %	Residential reviews %	Area X reviews %	Area Y reviews %	Area Z reviews %
Very important	18.9	44.1	21.4	13.8	24.1
Fairly important	28.8	29.4	34.3	28.7	22.2
Fairly unimportant	37.4	20.6	37.1	42.6	29.3
Very unimportant	14.9	5.9	7.1	14.9	26.1

reviews show that social workers felt that residential reviews were much more important; almost three-quarters of residential reviews were assessed as being important or very important in making decisions that would help to realise case work plans.

The range of the overall responses, as shown in Table 12.1 could be explained either by the variation in the nature of reviews or by the variation in the responses of different social workers. Examination of the responses of individual social workers did show that some variation was due to a tendency for individual social workers to regard reviews in general in different ways. (As indeed we saw in the earlier chapter on the functions of reviews.) However, a more important factor in explaining the spread of responses was the diverse character of reviews reflecting the particular circumstances of each case.

REVIEWS AND SOCIAL WORK

Our discussion so far suggests that reviews are not the primary decision-making forum - but are they regarded as important in other ways? Members of the social work area teams obviously felt that they were. Using a semi-structured questionnaire, their opinion was sought on the importance of reviews in several regards. Three questions were asked in relation to area reviews and residential reviews. These were "How would you assess the importance of reviews in regard to:

(i) the operation or management of the Social Services

Department
(ii)   the service provided for the client
(iii) your work in the Social Services Department."

The histograms in Figure 12.1 show the relative responses on a six-point scale from extremely important to extremely unimportant, for each of these three questions.

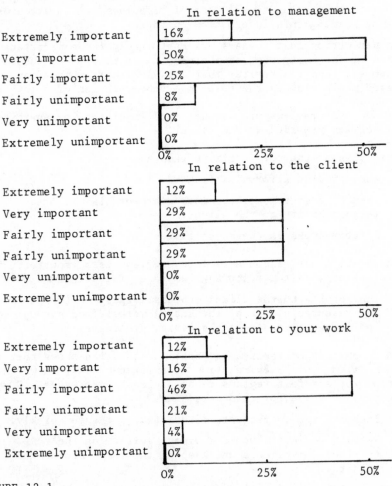

FIGURE 12.1
THE IMPORTANCE OF AREA REVIEWS

These responses show that social services team members see reviews to be important, particularly in relation to the management of the Social Services Department. Examples of the reasons given for this are:

145

They ensure that management are aware of the significant events in statutory cases, thus ensuring a degree of control.

They provide written proof that statutory obligations are being fulfilled, signed by the reviewing officer who has ultimate responsibility.

The management team may not be aware of all clients, social work inputs and lack of resources. They are a way of keeping this information up to date.

The perception that reviews are most likely to be important in terms of the management of the department reinforces the responses reported earlier that social workers most often viewed monitoring as the most important function of a review.

In general reviews are seen as less important in regard to the service provided to the client.

Examples of the more positive responses are:

They provide a formal safeguard.

They make social workers more aware of his ultimate responsibility to the client.

Effectiveness is the major issue.

However, other respondents found reviews less important, in this respect, as the following response illustrates

The service to the client depends largely on the goodwill and resourcefulness of the social worker, and not on the 'policing' elements of the review procedure.

A comparison of replies to the third question shows that this is the area, namely in relation to their own work, in which social workers felt reviews to be of least importance. Some of the reasons given for this were:

They are too infrequent, circumstances change quickly.

Without reviews I would envisage performing the same services for clients and keeping the same records and reports.

Other respondents did find reviews important in their work.

They help me identify areas of concern, to work out priorities and provide a readily available picture of planned future work.

They give management an idea of how we spend our time.

It should be noted that the Area Directors were much more

146

likely to see reviews as being extremely important.

Our respondents were asked the same three questions in relation to residential reviews. Their responses to these questions are shown in Figure 12.2.

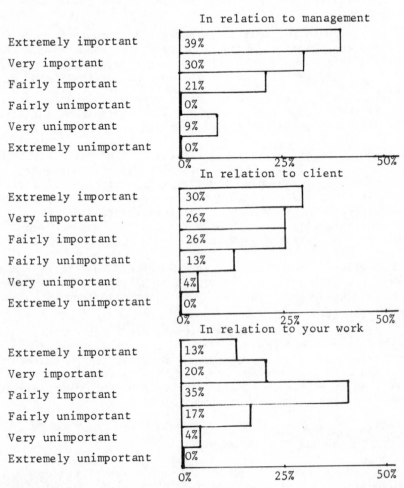

In relation to management

Extremely important	39%
Very important	30%
Fairly important	21%
Fairly unimportant	0%
Very unimportant	9%
Extremely unimportant	0%

In relation to client

Extremely important	30%
Very important	26%
Fairly important	26%
Fairly unimportant	13%
Very unimportant	4%
Extremely unimportant	0%

In relation to your work

Extremely important	13%
Very important	20%
Fairly important	35%
Fairly unimportant	17%
Very unimportant	4%
Extremely unimportant	0%

FIGURE 12.2
THE IMPORTANCE OF RESIDENTIAL REVIEWS

The range of responses in relation to residential reviews is wider than that for area reviews. However, the modal answer shows residential reviews are more often seen as extremely important. As with area reviews the importance of the review varies in relation to different aspects. Both area and residential reviews are seen as more important in relation to

different aspects. Both area and residential reviews are seen
as more important in relation to management of the Social
Services Department than to the service provided by the client
and least important to the work carried out by the social
worker.

The following replies represent most of the points made by
respondents.

> Children in residential care are subjected to more varied
> 'caring agents'. It is of primary importance that liaison
> and co-ordination are consolidated to present a consistent
> and 'tailor-made' environment for the particular child.

> Life in a children's home cannot go beyond 18 years and so,
> if there is no family support, it is most important that
> long-term decisions are made at reviews.

Although social workers were likely to find more residential
reviews extremely important, they also reported a greater
proportion as being unimportant or very unimportant. Social
workers often indicated to the researcher that they felt there
was a great range in the quality of residential reviews,
depending largely on which home was involved and who was
chairing the review.

Overall one could say that social workers felt reviews did
serve a useful purpose. Stevenson et al reported a very similar conclusion from their study of eight different social work
teams.

> For the most part, social workers tended to welcome formal
> reviews. They regarded them as important means of evalu-
> ating some of their caseload. Dissatisfaction was expres-
> sed when such reviews were regarded as merely administra-
> tive procedures and their professional functions were not
> developed. (Stevenson et al, 1978)

REVIEWS AND LONG TERM PLANNING

As we saw in Chapter 1 one of the main areas of concern in
child care practice is the poor performance of the social
services in planning for children in care. What did the
social workers involved in this study feel about this? They
were asked 'In general, how good is your social service
department at developing and recording long-term plans for the
children in its care or under its supervision?' Their
responses are shown in Table 12.2.

TABLE 12.2

LONG-TERM PLANNING	% OF ALL RESPONSES
Very good	4%
Good	29%
Satisfactory	46%
Poor	21%
Very poor	0

Nearly half of the respondents saw their own Social Services Department as only 'satisfactory' in making long-term plans. The range in responses is interesting. There was a difference in the responses of social workers from different area offices, but it was not particularly marked. Social workers in area X gave the highest rating, followed by those in area Z and then those in area Y. There were, however, major differences of opinion on this subject from individual social workers, within the same area office, as the following two quotes illustrate.

One social worker assessed the Social Services Department as 'good' and gave the following reason:

Plans are always discussed and agreed upon at an early stage in the case and thus afford a degree of direction and focus.

Another social worker from the same area office assessed the Social Services Department as 'poor'.

There is an inconsistent approach - plans change as different staff get involved - no overall policy is decided upon at the outset - everything is too fluid.

There were two recurring themes among the responses to the question of the standards of long-term planning:

a) that the situation was improving
b) that a lack of resources had an effect on the ability to plan.

The social workers' comments shown below represent these opinions:

It is improving, although I feel there is room for tighter requirements in respect of plans for children at an early stage of RIC rather than waiting for a review. This is beginning to happen, but perhaps it should become a requirement.

Longterm plans are oftern determined by available resources at the time rather than by careful planning.

Inconsistent staff ability and inadequacy of residential resources – more children's centres, more IT, more field workers and more specialisms within the latter, are required. You cannot plan successfully if you haven't got the appropriate components to choose from.

Resources often limit the practicality of plans and thus inhibit vision.

Having looked at long-term planning within the total work of the Social Services Department, we now want to consider it in relation to reviews. It has been suggested that reviews have the potential to play a major part in ensuring the developments of plans for all children. What picture emerges from this research of the role of reviews in planning in the research localities? Data which can help answer this were gathered in several ways. First social workers were asked, for each of their cases, 'How important was the review process in formulating plans?' The responses are shown in Table 12.3.

TABLE 12.3

IMPORTANCE OF THE REVIEW IN FORMULATING PLANS	% OF ALL RESPONSES
Very important	20.0
Fairly important	27.0
Fairly unimportant	35.2
Very unimportant	17.8

In a majority of cases social workers feel reviews are unimportant in formulating plans although the responses are spread throughout the range.

The second source of data was the researcher's assessment of the content of the review, with regard to discussion of the long-term objectives of each case.

The distribution of the researcher's assessment is shown in Table 12.4.

TABLE 12.4

LONG-TERM OBJECTIVES	% OF ALL REVIEWS ATTENDED
Assumed and not discussed	21.3
Reaffirmed	20.6
Re-examined	31.6
None of these	26.5

150

This points to long-term plans being actively discussed in less than one third of all reviews. This table also shows 21.3% and 20.6% of reviews as assuming or confirming existing plans for the child. These figures should be considered against data gathered from the case records.

In examining the case records of all the children whose reviews were included in this project, the researcher looked to see how far the case notes recorded long-term objectives. Long-term objectives were recorded in less than one quarter of all case records. This is not to say that the social worker does not have a long-term plan, but that this was 'carried in the head' rather than formulated and included in the case work file. If all those involved in a case are to work together surely these must be recorded. As Robinson found in his study of interaction between field and residential workers when planning for children:

> It is clear that there are generally differences between what the parties to care of a child, including the child, think should be happening to the child. (Robinson, 1981)

Awareness of such differences are more likely to emerge if the objectives of the case are not only discussed jointly, but are also recorded.

It would seem that reviews at present do not play a vital part in developing and monitoring long-term plans for children in care. From the responses to the questionnaires, backed up by informal discussion, it can be seen that many social workers are very aware of the need to improve planning and see a role for reviews in ensuring this. In particular social workers see planning as a collective exercise, where responsibility needs to be shared. If decisions were more frequently the product of collective discussion, social workers might feel less inhibited in recording such agreed decisions.

SUMMARY

What conclusions, on the importance of reviews, can we draw from the findings reported in this chapter? Firstly, although some major decisions are taken in reviews, the majority of major decisions in child care are taken outside the review process. Secondly, that there is a wide divergence, not to say confusion, expressed by individual social workers on the purpose of reviews and hence their importance in relation to different functions. Thirdly, that, in practice, the importance of reviews is seen to vary with individual cases. Fourthly, that social workers are aware of the need to improve long-term planning for children in care but are uncertain how

this relates to the present review process. Fifthly, that
members of social work area teams in general feel reviews are
important.

13 A way forward?

The broader context for this research project was established
in the first three chapters. In particular, Chapter 2 contained an examination of other studies relating to the review
process. The picture that emerged from these was not an
encouraging one. They demonstrated that many reviews were not
carried out within the regulation time limits, that many were
brief and limited in membership and that many were little more
than an administrative procedure.

Against this generally low standard for the country as a
whole, the results of this research show that Wainshire Social
Services Department organised their review process in an
efficient and orderly fashion. Overall 84% of reviews included
in the sample were conducted within six months of the previous
review, and a total of 96% were conducted within eight months.
It should also be noted that this Authority adopted a very
broad definition of 'reviewable cases'. Thus, as well as all
children in care, all children who were under supervision to
the authority or whose names were included on the 'at risk'
register were included in the review process.

The study also appears to demonstrate a very high level of
self-assessed implementation of review decisions by Wainshire
social workers (see Chapter 11). Social workers saw themselves
as having implemented 78.7% of all decisions and having
successfully achieved the aims implicit in the decision in
62.2% of cases. However, when the nature of these decisions
was examined, (as reported in Chapter 10) it was apparent that
the decisions were recorded in a very imprecise way. Rarely
was a time-scale for implementation included; both the goals
which the decisions were aiming to achieve and the action
necessary to achieve them were recorded, more often than not,
in an imprecise way. This lack of specificity in the decisions
makes a high level of assessed implementation inevitable.
Indeed this is a very similar result and conclusion to that
found by Festinger in her study of compliance with court
directives in judicial reviews in the USA (see page 20).

The original hypothesis that guided the design of this research related to the rate of implementation of review decisions. However, because of this very high level of decision implementation partial analysis of the relationship between this factor and a range of other variables is likely to prove less interesting than other implications from the research findings. One exception to that, is the investigation of the differential ratio of decision implementation depending on the place of the review. Comparisons were made between the review process in each of three social work area offices and in residential establishments within one Local Authority. Although there were some differences in the style and organisation and in the outputs from the reviews in each of the three areas, these differences were minor in comparison to the marked differences between all the reviews conducted in area offices and those conducted in Children's Homes. In comparison to area offices, reviews conducted in Children's Homes in Wainshire were likely to last longer, to include a larger number of people, to occasionally include the child (which never happened in area reviews), to adopt a more explicit decision-making approach, to make decisions which were more specific and which had a greater impact on the child. However, residential decisions were also less likely to be implemented and less likely to be successfully implemented.

Investigation of the causes of this non-implementation suggests that it is related to the nature of the decisions; 'residential' decisions were more likely to be important and significantly to affect the child's life and were more likely to have resource consequences. A full discussion of these factors and their implications has already been presented in Chapter 11.

It is not intended to include in this final chapter a repetition of the detailed research findings which have already been discussed. Rather, it is hoped to conclude this report by highlighting issues that have arisen from the research and which appear to be more widely applicable in their implications.

As we have seen, there was in Wainshire a review process that was administratively efficient. But this begs the question: administratively efficient to what purpose? The conducting of reviews, especially where a high proportion of the total area case load is included, entails a high opportunity cost for all those involved. There is, therefore, a need to ensure that the resultant outputs from the review process are of sufficient value to offset these costs. Any consideration of how these costs and outputs can be balanced raises many more questions than the initial one - 'are reviews conducted within the regulations?'. The results of this research raise four such issues, each of which are interrelated. These are: the purposes or functions of reviews; the quality of social work recording; the place of long-term planning for children in care; and participation by children and their families in the making of decisions which affect them.

THE PURPOSES OF REVIEWS

An examination of the writings related to reviews reveals that the purposes of reviews are often assumed but that there exists no concise or official statement which establishes these purposes explicitly. Empirical evidence was therefore sought on how reviews were being used in practice, and on how members of the review perceived the functions being fulfilled at each individual review. The results from this confirmed that reviews were serving several purposes and, furthermore that the particular combination of functions fulfilled varied with individual reviews.

Not only are reviews multifunctional, there is also a diversity of opinion among social workers as to the functions which reviews should perform and a degree of real confusion among many social workers on this issue. This confusion is most apparent when reviews conducted in area offices are compared with those in residential establishments. The organisation and character of these meetings are so different that they must be considered as distinctive types of discussion or decision-making mechanisms. Yet the statutory requirement which initiates each is basically the same.

Despite this uncertainty over the explicit purposes of reviews, it is worth noting that none of the social workers included in this sample believed that reviews should be abandoned. Although some social workers undoubtedly saw the outcome of reviews as having little significance, while still demanding of their time, there was nonetheless a strong residual sense that reviews perform a valuable function. Perhaps this belief mirrors that of social work activity as a whole, in that, while doubts may exist about its purpose, few serious commentators believe it does not have a real value.

Nonetheless it would seem that if the full potential of reviews is to be realised, those participating in the exercise must have a clearer understanding of why they are doing so. It is only when this has been accomplished that it is possible effectively to monitor how successfully these purposes or

objectives have been achieved. In this respect, we are
reminded of the relevance of the conclusions reached by
Martin, Fox and Murray on the Scottish Children's Hearings
(see page 18) 'If those who had designed the system had made
an unambiguous statement of its central objectives, it might
have been possible to assess empirically with what degree of
success this objective had been attained'.

Furthermore it is only after a clear understanding of the
purposes or functions has been reached that it is possible to
consider the most effective mechanism for achieving those
purposes. The functions of reviews and their organisation are
necessarily and intimately linked. From this it follows that
before the Secretary of State considers how best to implement
Section 3, para 7 (1) of the 1975 Children Act by introducing
regulations on the conduct of reviews he should first make
clear the objectives or purposes of the review process.
Specific suggestions on this are noted later.

THE QUALITY OF SOCIAL WORK RECORDING

As is apparent, this study did not set out to examine in
detail the methods or quality of social work recording. However, during the course of the study it was necessary to read
the case files on all the children included in the sample and
in particular to read the completed review forms. Recording in
social work is a topic which raises strong comment from workers.
Indeed it was this feeling of dissatisfaction with case
recording that prompted the members of BASW to press for the
establishment, in 1983, of a working party to examine the
topic. That working party concluded:

> We consider, then, that a radical reappraisal of the role
> and organisation of record systems in social work is
> needed. (BASW, 1983)

The present study offers only limited 'evidence' for such a
debate; nonetheless the quality of recording in general and of
reviews in particular does influence the review process and
therefore impinges on the research findings. There were two
respects in particular in which this was a significant factor:
the inclusion in case records of the objectives or plans for
each child, and the quality of the recording of review
decisions.

While it was by no means true for all cases, the general
picture gathered from reading case records and attending
reviews was of a lack of clearly stated case objectives. Case
objectives may well have been raised between the senior and

the social worker in supervision sessions, but more often than not the discussion in a review was not related to any such formulated or recorded statement of objectives. The need for such a statement of objectives has long been recognised and indeed has been taken a step further in the concept of 'contracts', or written agreements. The term 'contract' is most often associated with special fostering for teenagers and as the survey by Shaw & Hipgrave (1983) shows a high proportion (86%) of all special fostering schemes use some form of written contract. The word contract presupposes some form of voluntary agreement between parties who are equally free to negotiate and accept the terms of the agreement. This is rarely the case in child care, so written agreements or understandings may be a more appropriate terminology. As we noted in Chapter 2, BASW certainly believe that all placements of children in care should be based on written agreements between all the parties involved. Similarly, those who believe in the 'philosophy of permanence' see written agreements as an essential part of the relationship between the social services agency and the family. In this way the social services department can be honest with the family while at the same time bringing them into the decision-making arena. In explaining the use of written agreements White goes on to point out that:

> Ultimately the most important justification for this approach to work, however, must be the fact that such research as has been done suggests that parents working within the clear guidelines of a document such as I have described are more successful in continuing to care for their child or in having the child restored to them. (White, 1983)

Examples of the application of this type of approach in the London Borough of Lambeth were presented by Chris Hussell (1983). He suggests that any written agreement or understanding should contain the following statements:

1. What the problems are in terms of the welfare of the child.
2. What it is intended to achieve.
3. What social services can do to help.
4. What the client will do or is expected to do.
5. What the consequences of success or failure are likely to be.

Compared with examples of practice like this from other authorities the limited emphasis to be found in Wainshire on the recording of case objectives is striking. The inclusion in a case record, or on a review form of a statement of objectives provides the necessary basis for a review

effectively to evaluate work to date and to plan future work.
The lack of recorded objectives encourages reviews to follow a
narrow or retrospective time-scale and to engage in information
exchange, or low level monitoring rather than evaluative
reassessments.

A second aspect of recording, already noted above, is the
lack of precision with which many of the review decisions
were recorded. Details of the findings generated by the
application of a typology of review decisions, and the implications of these, have already been discussed. However, in
assessing the value of the review system the quality of
recording is a point worthy of serious consideration. As with
the recording of case objectives, a lack of precision in
recording a review decision means there is not a sufficiently
sound base for evaluating the implementation of that decision,
which must therefore reduce the potential value of subsequent
reviews. Furthermore, imprecise decision making and recording
may lead to a blurring of the intentions implicit in the
decisions and thus reduce any sense of urgency in implementation. In this context one is reminded once again of the
warning included in 'Foster Care: A Guide to Practice':'Unless
reviews decide 'what, how and who' plans tend to remain written
hopes on case records' (DHSS, 1976).

LONG-TERM PLANNING

Although the major characteristic of the current debate on
child care policy is the disagreements that have been expressed
over the role and powers of the local authority, there is
concurrently a large measure of consensus over the need to
improve the planning of social work with or on behalf of children and their families.

Much of the rationale for the formulation of such plans has
already been rehearsed in this chapter in the section dealing
with the recording of case objectives. In some cases very
specific plans may be appropriate, in others less detailed yet
clearly stated aims or objectives may be sufficient, or all
that is possible. Although the end product may vary in its
level of specificity, the making of a plan enables the social
worker to adopt a more decisive approach to casework and
therefore to reduce the amount of crisis orientated, reactive
decision making. The research findings that have been presented in this report arose from three different approaches to
the topic of long-term planning. These were:

- social workers' opinions on the importance of long-term
  planning and their satisfaction with the performance

of their own department in this respect.
- the evidence derived from the observation of review discussions as to the existence of such plans.
- the appropriateness of the development of long-term plans as a function of statutory reviews.

In practice, some attempt at long-term planning was by no means universal in the cases included in this study. Furthermore, social work staff, while aware of a general need to improve planning, displayed a considerable diversity of views over the form and the methods of achieving this.

Some social worker respondents explained this ambivalence towards long-term planning as deriving from practical considerations, rather than from concern over any diminution of clients' rights. These practical considerations had two dimensions. One was the highly volatile nature of many cases, leading to constant and unpredictable changes of circumstances. The other factor which was perceived as a practical limitation on effective long-term planning was the lack of appropriate resources whereby the making and implementation of individually tailored plans could become a reality. In summary it can be said that the review system as conducted in Wainshire did not play a large part in the formulation of long-term plans, nor was there any consensus that this was an appropriate function for the reviews to fulfil; yet there was an expression of both the need and desire to improve this aspect of practice. To specifically charge the statutory review with the task of monitoring, or reassessing, plans for each child might not only give an emphasis to an early formulation of plans, it might also establish the necessary framework for a positive approach to case work with the child and his family.

PARTICIPATION IN REVIEWS

The submissions to the House of Commons Select Committee which related to the formulation and implementation of regulations on the conduct of reviews laid great stress on the need to involve children in the review process in order to fulfil the duty placed upon Local Authorities to ascertain the wishes and feelings of children in their care. The findings of the research show that children were only very occasionally included in reviews in Wainshire; natural parents and foster parents were included even less often. The pattern in Wainshire is therefore one of minimal participation by children and young people in the decision-making process. However, one must consider whether a statutory obligation to include children or young people in their reviews is necessarily the best way of ensuring that they are actually involved in the

decision-making process. There are a number of reasons for
adopting a cautious attitude.

First, simply to invite a child to attend a case conference
style of review, which is the usual format for children in
residential care, may not in fact involve him in decision-
making. As a result of experimenting with a new review system
to include children, the Jensons point to the need for small
intimate reviews, rather than the usual large case conference.
Their reasons for this are:

> To expose a child to such a group, which is normally a
> fairly formal situation, would be to expose the child to
> a threatening experience. Most children under such
> circumstances would be inhibited from offering a proper
> contribution. (Jenson & Jenson, 1978)

However, participation or involvement in reviews can take
place in other ways than by simply allowing children to attend
and expecting them to contribute to the discussion. Involvement may be through the nomination of a friendly spokes-
person, or through prepared statements or notes. In writing
of experiments in a Church of England Children's Home, Pamela
Skinner notes that:

> Of the methods of involvement which were suggested, by
> far the most successful in terms of enabling the children
> to express feelings, was in the use of a form or question-
> naire. They were able to write things that they could not
> verbalise directly to people. (Skinner, 1980)

It is certainly reasonable to assume that opening the review
process to children and their families would stimulate the
need to question afresh many of the assumptions held about the
purposes, organisation and outcomes of reviews. There is,
however, another aspect to the question of how best to
ascertain the wishes and feelings of children in relation to
decisions which affect them. If it is hoped that this obligation will be fulfilled by including children in reviews, this
is to ignore those decision-making instances that occur outside the review process. This study has demonstrated that
reviews are only one forum for making decisions and certainly
not the most important one:- less than one-quarter of all the
important decisions taken in these cases were taken in reviews.
Consequently the inclusion of children in reviews would not in
itself fulfil the obligation to involve them fully in decision-
making. Mechanisms to include children in reviews may appear
to be a relatively simple exercise; to include them in all
decision-making occasions will require other consultative
devices. The issue of participation in statutory reviews ought
not to detract from the wider problem of meaningful involvement.

A third factor which arises from any proposal to enlarge the composition of the review is the organisational implications, particularly for reviews which are conducted as were the area office reviews in this study. The impact of such a change as this on the work of Area Y has already been speculated upon (see page 81). In the present resource climate it may only be possible to enlarge the membership or to conduct reviews more thoroughly by first categorising them and then establishing a system of priorities. This would mean that all cases would be subject to at least a basic form of review (which may be all that is happening at present) but priority cases would be accorded greater attention and fuller participation.

A WAY FORWARD

Given the findings from this research and the implications that have been drawn from these, what is the way forward for reviews? In order to answer that question it is necessary first to answer a series of interrelated questions: - what is the purpose or purposes of reviews?; what are the organisational regulations that will enable reviews to best fulfil these purposes?; should reviews be prioritised to allow for broader and more detailed discussions when necessary? What follows are suggestions for answering these questions.

The fact that the standards of organisation and conduct of reviews in Wainshire compares favourably with the generally unsatisfactory national picture, serves to underline the need to establish more effective national guidelines to ensure that standards can be raised for all authorities. This can probably best be achieved through the implementation of the 1975 Children Act relating to the regulation of reviews. However, if regulation of the conduct of reviews is to be used constructively, then there is a need for much greater clarity about the primary functions of reviews. As the functions and the processes of reviews are intimately related, developments in the conduct of reviews must be in relation to their primary functions. What then are the main options available to decision-makers who - at local or national level - wish to improve the quality of reviews?

There would seem to be five possible directions for development, relating to perceptions of the primary function of reviews. The principal functions are as follows.

1. Reviews can be the main source of <u>managerial infor-mation</u> - the route of communication between field-workers and management and between fieldworkers and residential staff and management.

2. Reviews can play a key part in <u>supervision,</u> in the monitoring of casework as a whole.
3. Reviews can be used to <u>monitor the making of decisions</u> to ensure that effective plans are developed for children in care.
4. Reviews can be used to monitor the <u>implementation of decisions.</u>
5. Reviews can be used as the <u>primary route for partici-pation</u> by children and their families in the making and monitoring of decisions which affect or determine their lives.

Although reviews may be capable of fulfilling more than one function at a time, there is a real danger in letting them remain 'as all things to all men', as is the case at present. The development of statutory reviews will only be beneficial to child care practice if there is greater clarity about the purposes they are aiming to fulfil. Therefore there needs to be some measure of selectivity so that priority can be given to the development of reviews in certain ways. Which of these five possible functions should be given most emphasis?

A managerial or participative emphasis?

The traditional role of reviews has been broadly managerial. A recent emphasis has been on increasing the participation of clients in decision-making, including reviews. If partici-pation is to increase this is likely to lead to a style of review more akin to a case conference. However, the defining characterisitic of reviews is that they are scheduled at fixed intervals throughout the career of the child in care whereas participative involvement would be more appropriate at points of crisis and decision-making and these would not necessarily coincide with the review timetable. Therefore, it may be more appropriate to retain reviews as an explicitly managerial device, while advocating an increased use of informal discussions and case conferences to increase partici-pation by children and their families when important decisions are to be made. However, to ensure that an increased level of participation in decision-making actually occurred it may be necessary to make one of the explicit tasks allocated to reviews that of monitoring the extent to which clients had been involved in decision-making and the discussion of case-work objectives and strategies.

The primary function

This work and that of others quoted in the literature suggests that two of the greatest weaknesses in present child care practice are the limited emphasis on long-term planning for children in care and the failure to make appropriate and implementable decisions. Using reviews primarily for decision-making would not necessarily improve this. Rather than expecting reviews to be a primary forum for decision-making, they could make a greater contribution by monitoring the nature and quality of all child care decision-making and by monitoring the implementation of these decisions. There would therefore seem to be very good reasons for issuing regulations which would clearly place these functions at the centre of the review process. Such regulations would need to be designed to ensure that the reviewing officer was in no doubt that, at the end of each review, he or she should have satisfactory answers to a set of key questions on each case. The following four questions are an illustration of the direction these would need to take.

1. Has a long-term plan or set of objectives been clearly stated for the child?
2. Has the decision-making process been appropriate to the nature of the case? For example, have the child and his family been appropriately consulted and involved; has adequate consultation and discussion taken place within and across agency boundaries?
3. Have the objectives been specified appropriately and translated into decisions in such a manner that their implementation can be systematically monitored? For example, does the social worker and his/her supervisor have a clear understanding of how these objectives are to be pursued? Have the decisions been specified sufficiently precisely? Has the expected time-scale for implementation of each decision been recorded?
4. Has marked progress towards implementation of the decisions been achieved since the last review? Is there good reason to believe, for example, that the decisions can be implemented successfully and the objectives achieved? Have alternative objectives and decisions been formulated, should the first option become unobtainable?

In this way the purpose of reviews would become clearly specified. Moreover, by placing these key questions at the centre of the review process we would move towards a position in which both decision-making and managerial supervision were monitored.

Prioritising reviews

If reviews followed this form, it may be considered appropriate that the Reviewing Officer should not be part of the social work area team. An alternative could be the use of a specialist child care officer, or group, responsible at authority level for 'planning for children in care'. However, the use of such an officer or group may not be thought appropriate or necessary for all reviews, which returns us to an earlier point about the need to prioritise reviews.

If reviews were reoriented in the way suggested above - concentrating the focus on the nature and quality of decision-making - most reviews could proceed much as at present without entailing any substantial changes in their organisation. However, in a proportion of cases the adoption of this more rigorous review would require a more detailed approach and would require an increase in the time and effort expended. It is for this reason that one needs to prioritise reviews and carefully to select those situations where greater expenditure of time and effort is thought necessary. Guidelines on this may suggest that a more rigorous review is necessary, for instance, in the following situations: shortly after reception into care; following the breakdown of a placement; before a court hearing or change in legal status; before a child moves or leaves school; before any planned change in parental contact.

Statutory reviews have the potential to encourage high standards of child care practice. This potential is not being realised at present because of a lack of clarity about the purpose of reviews. It is suggested, therefore, that the primary focus of reviews should be the monitoring of the nature and quality of decision-making for children in care, together with the implementation of decisions. In this way the review can bring together the monitoring of decision-making and managerial supervision in all cases and offer a more stringent check on developments in selected situations.

References

ABAFA, (1979), Terminating Parental Contact, London.

Adcock, M., (1981), 'The Right of a Child to a Permanent Placement', in Rights of Children, BAAF, London.

Adcock, M., White, R., Rowlands, O., (1982), 'The Role of the Local Authority as a Parent', Adoption and Fostering, Vol.6, No.4, 1982.

Adcock, M., White, R., Rowlands, O., (1983), The Administrative Parent, BAAF, London.

Adoption and Fostering, (1980), 'Reviews', Editorial, Adoption and Fostering, No.99, No.1 of 1980.

Adoption and Fostering, (1981), 'Implementing the Children Act of 1975', Adoption and Fostering, No.103.

Aldgate, J. (1977), 'Identification of Factors Influencing Children's length of Stay in Care', unpublished PhD thesis, University of Edinburgh.

Aldgate, J., (1980), 'Identification of factors influencing children's length of stay in care', in Triseliotis, J. (Ed) New Developments in Foster Care and Adoption, Routledge & Kegan Paul.

Ashton, E.T., (1974) 'Making up your mind', Social Work Today, Vol.5, No.14, 17.10.74.

Barclay Report (1982), Social Workers: Their Roles and Tasks, Bedford Square Press, London.

Benson, J.K., (1973), 'The analysis of bureaucratic-professional conflict: functional versus dialectical approaches', Sociological Quarterly, Vol.14.

Brewer, C. and Lait, J., (1980), Can Social Work Survive, Temple Smith.

Brill, K., (1976), 'Positive thinking for children', Social Work Today, Vol.8, No.6, 9:11:76.

British Association of Social Workers,(1982), Guidelines for Practice in Family Placement, BASW, Birmingham.

British Association of Social Workers,(1983), Evidence to House of Commons Social Services Committee Inquiry into Children in Care, BASW, Birmingham.

British Association of Social Workers, (1983), Effective and Ethical Recording, BASW, Birmingham.

Castle, R.L., (1976), Case Conferences: A Cause for Concern, NSPCC Publications, London.

Child Poverty Action Group, (1975), The Children Bill: Rescue or Prevention, CPAG, London.

Children's Legal Centre, (1983), Children in Care - The Need for change, London.

Community Care, (1983), 'Outsiders to help make SSD's efficient', Community Care, 21.4.83, p.2.

Curtis Report, (1946), Report of the Care of Children Committee, Cmd 6922, HMSO, London.

Davies, C. (1983), 'Professionals in bureaucracies: the conflict thesis revisited', in Dingwall, R. and Lewis, P. (Eds) The Sociology of the Professions, Macmillan, London.

Davis, L., (1982), 'How long do we tolerate this nonsense?', Community Care, 7.1.82, p.15.

DHSS, (1974), Report of the Committee of Inquiry into the Care and Supervision Provided in Relation to Maria Colwell, HMSO.

DHSS, (1976), LAC(76) 15, 'Children Act 1975 ; Programme for Implementation'.

DHSS, (1976), Foster Care: A Guide to Practice, HMSO.

DHSS, (1982), A Study of the Boarding Out of Children, Social Work Service, 1982.

DHSS, (1983), LAC(83) 14, 'Personal Social Service Records - disclosure of information to clients'.

Drezner, S.M., (1973), 'The emerging art of decision-making', Social Casework, Vol.54, No.1, January, 1973.

Eckstein, H., (1969), 'Planning:the National Health Service', in Rose, R. (Ed) Policy-making in Britain, Macmillan, London.

Etzioni, A., (1968), The Active Society, Collier-Macmillon.

Etzioni, A., (1969), The Semi-Professionals and their Organisations, Free Press, New York.

Festinger, T.B., (1975), 'The New York Court review of children in foster care', Child Welfare, Vol.54, No.4, April 1975.

Festinger, T.B., (1976) 'The impact of the New York court review of children in foster care, Child Welfare, Vol.55, No.8 September 1976.

Fox, L., (1982), 'Two value positions in recent child care law and practice', British Journal of Social Work, Vol.12, No.3, June 1982.

Goldberg, E.M. and Warburton, R.W., (1979), Ends and Means in social work, Allen and Unwin.

Goldberg, E.M. and Connelly, W. (Eds), (1981), Evaluative Research in Social Care, Heinemann.

Goldstein, J., Freud, A. and Solnit, A., (1973), Beyond the Best Interests of the Child, Free Press, New York, Collier-Macmillon, London.

Hall, R.H. (1975), 'The Professions' in Occupations and the Social Structure, Englewood Cliffs, New Jersey, Prentice-Hall.

Hallett, C. and Stevenson, O., (1980), Child Abuse: Aspects of Intreprofessional Co-operation, Allen and Unwin, London.

Hazel, N., (1981), A Bridge to Independence, Basil Blackwell.

Hazel, N., (1982), 'The Regulation of family placement', Adoption and Fostering, Vol.6, No.3, 1982.

Hardiker, P. and Barker, M., (1981), Theories of Practice in Social Work, Academic Press, London.

Hill, M.J., (1972), The Sociology of Public Administration, Weidenfeld and Nicolson, London.

Holden, A., (1980), Children in Care, Comyn Books.

Holman, R., (1975), 'The place of fostering in social work', British Journal of Social Work, Vol.5, No.1, 1975.

Holman, R., (1976 and 1980), Inequality in Child Care, CPAG, London.

Home Office, (1965), The Child, the Family and the Young Offender, Cmnd 2742, HMSO.

Home Office, (1968), Children in Trouble, Cmnd 3001, HMSO.

Houghton Report, (1972), Report of the Departmental Committee on the Adoption of Children, Cmnd 5107, HMSO.

Howells, J.G. (1974), Remember Maria, Butterworths.

Hussell, C., (1983), 'Understanding Contracts', Adoption and Fostering, Vol.7, No.3.

Ingleby Report, (1960), Report of the Committee on Children and Young Persons, Cmnd 1191, HMSO.

Jenson, G. and Jenson, L. (1978), 'Reassuring Reviews', Community Care, 11:10:78.

Jordan, B., (1974), Poor Parents, Routledge & Kegan Paul.

Levin, P.H., (1972), 'On decision and decision-making', Public Administration, Vol.50, Spring 1972.

Lindblom, C.E., (1968), The Policy Making Process, Prentice-Hall.

Lipsky, M., (1980), Street Level Bureaucracy, Russell Sage Foundation, New York.

March, J.G. and Simon, H.A., (1958), Organisations, Wiley.

Martin, F. and Murray, K.,(1976), Children's Hearings, Scottish Academic Press.

Martin , F., Fox, S. and Murray, S., (1981), Children Out of Court, Scottish Academic Press.

McVeigh, J., (1982), Gaskin, Jonathan Cape, 1982.

Murray, N., (1982), 'Contrary to Natural Justice', Community Care, 29:7:82.

National Association of Young People in Care, (1983), Sharing Care, NAYPIC.

North Area Research Group, (1981), 'Monitoring Reception into Care', Adoption and Fostering, 104, No.2 of 1981.

Packman, J., (1981), The Child's Generation, second edition, Basil Blackwell and Martin Robertson.

Page, R. and Clark, G.A., (1977), Who Cares?, National Children's Bureau, London.

Parker, R.A., (1971), Planning for Deprived Children, National Children's Home.

Parker, R.A., (1980), (ed), Caring for Separated Children, Macmillan.

Parsloe, P., (1981), Social Service Area Teams, George Allen and Unwin.

Payne, M., (1979), Power, Authority and Responsibility in the Social Services, Macmillan.

Pierson, J., (1983), 'The American Way', Community Care, 13:10: 1983.

Read, J., (1981), Child Care Career Planning, Essex County Council.

Robinson, J., (1981), Planning for Children in Care, Buckingham County Council.

Rowbotham, R., Hey, A. and Billis, D., (1974), Social Service Departments, Heinemann.

Rowe, J. and Lambert, L., (1973), Children who Wait, ABAFA, London.

Rowe, J., Hundleby, M., Paul, H. and Keane, A., (1981), 'The Influence of Section 29', Adoption and Fostering, No.103.

Rowe, J., Cain, H., Hundleby, M. and Keane, A., (1984), Long-term fostering and the Children Act, BAAF, London.

Sayer, P., Forbes, D., Newman, P., and Jamison, T., (1976), 'Positive Planning for Children in Care', Social Work Today,

12:10:76.

Shaw, M. and Hipgrave, T., (1983), Specialist Fostering, Batsford Academic in association with BAAF.

Sheldon, B., (1982), 'A Measure of Success', Social Work Today, Vol.13, No.21, 2:2:82.

Simon, H.A., (1957), Administrative Behaviour, Macmillon, New York.

Simon, H.A., (1965), 'The New Science of management decision', in The Shape of Automation for Men and Management, Harper & Row.

Sinclair, R., (1982), 'Include them Out', Community Care, 12:8:82.

Sinclair, R. and Webb, A., (1982), 'Care on the Dole', Social Work Today, Vol.14, No.10, 9:11:82.

Sinclair, R., (1983), 'The functions of reviews', Adoption and Fostering, Vol.7, No.2.

Sinclair, R., (1983), 'The nature of the decisions taken at reviews', Adoption and Fostering, Vol.7, No.4, 1983.

Sinclair, R., (1983), 'Do they do what they say they will do?', Community Care, 22:12:83.

Skinner, P., (1980), 'Our experiment in involving children in reviews', Social Work Service, No.22.

Social Work Today, (1981), 'A share in care', Social Work Today, Vol.13, No.16, 8:12:81.

Smith, G., (1979), Social Work and the Sociology of Organisations, Routledge & Kegan Paul.

Smith G. and Ames, J., (1976), 'Area Teams in Social Work', British Journal of Social Work, Vol.6, No.1, 1976.

Smith G. and May, D., (1980), 'Executing decisions in the Children's Hearings', Sociology, Vol.14, No.4, November 1980.

Stein, M. and Ellis, S., (1983), 'Wallflowers at their own reviews', Community Care, 8:9:83.

Stein, M. and Ellis, S., (1983), Gizza Say, NAYPIC.

Stevenson, et al, (1978), <u>Social Service Teams: the Practi-</u>tioner's view, DHSS, HMSO.

Thorpe, R., (1974), 'Mum and Mrs So and So', <u>Social Work Today</u>, Vol.6, No.22.

White, R., (1983), 'Written agreements with families', <u>Adoption and Fostering</u>, Vol.7, No.4.

Wilding, P., (1982), <u>Professional Power and Social Welfare</u>, Routledge & Kegan Paul.

Wilson, H., (1974), 'Parenting in poverty', <u>British Journal of Social Work</u>, Vol.4, No.3, Autumn 1974.